"What an inspiring collection of stories from eight uniquely called and gifted leaders! Each one shows us how God empowers women to lead others in the right direction."

—**Liz Curtis Higgs, best-selling author of** *The Girl's Still Got It*

"I'm not sure how well, if at all, the eight women whose voices and stories make up this volume know each other, but together they form a remarkable sisterhood. Their stories of hard-won wisdom, persevering faith, restoring grace, and—always—the God who wastes nothing are riveting, invigorating, poignant and, sometimes, very funny. This book is for anyone—man or woman—who is or is becoming a leader and who needs bread for the journey: you just stumbled on a whole bakery."

—**Mark Buchanan, author of** *The Rest of God*

"As a television host and interviewer I've read scores of books and interviewed scores of authors on leadership. Generally they are prescriptive and generic, restating the obvious. This is not the case with *Faith, Life and Leadership*. The great appeal of the book is that the various authors share lessons learned from real-life experiences, some of them tragic. There are more tears than theories. I found the read refreshingly compelling, uplifting and inspiring. Not your typical leadership book. It's a keeper."

—**Jim Cantelon, author and host of** *Jim Cantelon Today*

"Christian leadership is an imperative in today's world. The faith journeys of the accomplished women who tell their stories in this book are excellent examples of such leadership and deserve our full attention. Their insights into leadership are well worth reading and taking to heart."

—**Preston Manning, founder and president of the Manning Centre**

"God uniquely grants to each person the appointed time to speak into our culture about human dignity, social responsibility and the transforming power of fulfilling one's calling. Stories are powerful communicators and the eight women featured in this timely book have been open with their leadership journeys. They have stood their ground and braved some of life's biggest challenges, and yet they have done so with passion and determination, seizing opportunities, and making an impact around them."

—**Bruce Clemenger, president of the Evangelical Fellowship of Canada**

"*Faith, Life and Leadership* tells the true stories of eight extraordinary Canadian women who said 'Yes' to fulfilling their calling and purpose. With honesty, biblical truth and powerful illustrations, the authors reveal their journeys to leadership—the obstacles faced and the lessons learned. This book will inspire and encourage you, but it will also challenge you to live up to your highest potential as a woman of God. I highly recommend it."

—**Carol Kent, international speaker and author of *Speak Up with Confidence***

"These incredibly honest stories of God disciplining leaders over a lifetime will help both men and women become godly, Spirit-led leaders."

—**John Pellowe, CEO of Canadian Council of Christian Charities**

*Faith, Life and Leadership: 8 Canadian Women Tell Their Stories* is a project of:

# WOMEN TOGETHER
## www.women-together.org

# Faith, Life & Leadership

## 8 CANADIAN WOMEN TELL THEIR STORIES

General Editor, Georgialee Lang

**FOREWORD BY DR BRIAN STILLER,**
Global Ambassador, World Evangelical Alliance

Published by: Castle Quay Books
Tel: (416) 573-3249
E-mail: info@castlequaybooks.com
www.castlequaybooks.com

 CASTLE QUAY BOOKS

Edited by Marina Hofman Willard, and Lori Mackay
Cover and book interior by Burst Impressions
Printed at Essence Printing, Belleville, Ontario

"Wildflower" is written by David Richardson and Doug Edwards. Copyright Edsel Music 1972, renewed 2000. Used by permission. Administered by Nettwerk One Music (Canada) Ltd. www.wildflowersong.com
Portions of Carolyn's chapter were adapted with permission from Carolyn's books *Wrestling with Angels* (Harvest House/ConversantLife.com) and *Theology in Aisle Seven* (CTE Books).

Unless otherwise marked, Scripture is taken from The Holy Bible, English Standard Version. ESV® Permanent Text Edition® (2016). Copyright © 2001 by Crossway Bibles, a publishing ministry of Good News Publishers. • Scripture quotations marked (MSG) are taken from The Message. Copyright © 1993, 1994, 1995, 1996, 2000, 2001, 2002. Used by permission of NavPress Publishing Group. • Holy Bible, New International Version®, NIV® Copyright ©1973, 1978, 1984, 2011 by Biblica, Inc.® Used by permission. All rights reserved worldwide. • Scripture quotations marked (WEB) are taken from the World English Bible which is in the Public Domain.

Foreword by Dr. Brian Stiller

**Library and Archives Canada Cataloguing in Publication**

**Lang, Georgialee, author**
     Faith, life and leadership : 8 Canadian women tell their
stories / Georgialee Lang.

ISBN 978-1-927355-81-7 (paperback)

     1. Leadership--Religious aspects--Christianity.  2. Christian
women--Religious life--Canada.  3. Christian women--Canada--
Biography.  4. Christian biography--Canada.  I. Title.

BV4597.53L43L36 2016          248.8'43          C2016-905798-4

# Foreword

I came to Christian faith as a teenager after listening to Bernice Gerard preach. Grace Brown led me into a Pentecostal experience, and May English taught me how to preach. My father, a "bishop" of churches, noted that in churches unable to survive, an obvious solution was a female pastor: they seemed to have the skills to get churches on track. How privileged I was in my family and church to learn early the equal gifting of the Spirit in ministry.

There are many reasons why it has taken so long for us to understand the gifting of God's people in ways that aren't to be distinguished by gender. What I do know is that missions over the past century of our history have been carried out in good part by women who have gone to some of the most difficult places, and under the most trying circumstances, with the message of Christ.

What we have in this book, *Faith, Life and Leadership: 8 Canadian Women Tell Their Stories*, are open commentaries of those who defied old forms of resistance that tragically kept many from entering into the fulfillment of their gifting and calling. Instead, these stories will help open roads for travel, uncover vistas for seeing, unlock doors to ministry and create new lives to live. What creative and action-inducing stories.

I know of no other Canadian book that brings together such a selection of women who in life and ministry are exceptionally gifted, serving Christ and His church in ways remarkable and contemporary. What a listing, all beginning with Lorna and Marg in conversation.

I had begun a new Canadian magazine, *Faith Today*, and was looking for writers when I bumped into the writings of Lorna Dueck. We met in Winnipeg, and in time I introduced her to David Mainse, who was looking for a co-host for his daily *100 Huntley Street* program. She had the skills and the determination. From there, her combined ability and resolute spirit carried her into her own weekly national television show and on into managing the Christian Crossroads Communication network.

Margaret Gibb, like Lorna, is determined and restless, looking for ways to express her faith outside of the usual pastoral and ministerial opportunities. Taking on the ministry of Women Alive, Marg is an example of a person who some thought would be sidelined by gender but instead refused to let gender define her gifting and calling. Today, the same determined and restless spirit has begun a new ministry called Women Together, which impacts not just women here, but also women around the world.

As you read your way through these testimonials, you will be struck, as was I, by their candour and openness to tell us about their journeys. This rich treasury sets a new threshold on which a coming generation will take their cue. A history of the Canadian church is in your hands.

Enjoy the texture of their words, the moisture of their tears and the windows of grace their personal stories open to us as we follow in faith, opened by their pictures of God's loving ways.

**Dr. Brian C. Stiller**
**Global Ambassador, The World Evangelical Alliance**

## Acknowledgements

The Church father Augustine once said, "No one can walk alone." Indeed, in every story there are thousands of smaller stories involving people who were part of discovery, learning, growing and becoming. The people named in this book are mentioned because of their integral part of the development process of the authors, yet we acknowledge that hundreds could be added. Our stories are much bigger than we are.

Special thanks to Aileen Van Ginkel and Natasha Lichti, who helped our stories come alive through their editorial help. And a big expression of appreciation to our publishers, Larry and Marina Willard of Castle Quay Books, who saw the need for this book and encouraged us to be real and authentic in our storytelling as an encouragement to leaders on the same journey.

**Georgialee Lang**
**Margaret Gibb**

## Editor's Note

E very dream starts as an idea—a seed thought—that requires time to incubate, sprout and grow. The idea for a book on Canadian women in leadership, their stories and life lessons, germinated from discussions between Lorna Dueck and Margaret Gibb over ten years ago. "Wouldn't it be great if..." guided their conversations, culminating in the conviction that a book on faith-driven leadership would be a gift of encouragement to women who found themselves blessed and challenged with opportunities they never expected.

In the summer of 2014, a newsfeed on social media caught my attention. Margaret Gibb was coming to Kelowna, British Columbia, where my husband and I spend our summers. All I knew about Margaret was that she was a well-respected Christian leader from Ontario. I also knew I had to meet her.

As we sat in the warm Okanagan sunshine, we felt an immediate kinship and, as women often do, began sharing our lives—our experiences, our challenges and our hopes and dreams for the future. One of her dreams matched one I had nurtured for several years: to assemble a group of Canadian women to share their stories—their journeys of faith, life and leadership.

We envisioned stories of ordinary women who stepped out of their comfort zones to achieve extraordinary accomplishments but received so much more. We could never have imagined the panoply of life and leadership journeys that emerged and the recurring themes that ran through their pages of transparent narrative.

Our contributors come from diverse walks of life and professional roles, including politics, law, entertainment, social services and non-profit sectors. Their paths to leadership unite them as they share stories of grappling with confidence and self-esteem, pursuing excellence through lifelong learning and education, balancing career and family life and overcoming failures.

One theme arises above the others, and that is the simple truth that it is through God's grace that each of these women overcame stumbling blocks to persist and pursue their dreams and, along the way, became leaders.

**Georgialee Lang**

# *Communicating*

## on a Faith Frequency

Lorna Dueck

I was in the womb of a mother who made desperate attempts to have an abortion. I was abandoned in a crib, faced rejection and abuse, was screamed at as garbage and beaten up as the unwanted intruder. Now I live as a deeply loved child of God, daughter, wife, mother and communicator. It's been a remarkable road. If anyone needs evidence that God loves and pursues people, pick me.

I'm responding to the invitation to write out my own story of becoming a leader. I'm writing while on sabbatical, a delightful pause earned through one of the consequences of leadership: fatigue. I heartily agree with J. Oswald Sanders in his excellent book *Spiritual Leadership: A Commitment to Excellence for Every Believer* where he wrote, "If a Christian is not willing to rise early and work late, to expend greater effort in diligent study and faithful work, that person will not change a generation. Fatigue is the price of leadership. Mediocrity is the result of never getting tired."[1]

---

[1] J. Oswald Sanders, *Spiritual Leadership: A Commitment to Excellence for Every Believer* (Chicago: Moody Publishers, n.d.), 119.

By 2015, mine was a rather happy fatigue—not a maddening burnout but just a growing realization that, mentally and emotionally, I was pushing myself harder than I had ever done in 21 years of media witness for Christianity. I had learned from so many wonderful leaders along my journey. I had interviewed people of many varieties for radio and TV, written articles and produced documentaries, blogs, Facebook posts and tweets on hundreds of life stories and news events. For over 20 years I had been looking journalistically for "the God angle," and the stories had overwhelmingly reminded me that God loves humanity, and God loves me.

So in this three-month window of my sabbatical pause, it's a gift to reflect back and think deeper about my path into leadership. Three themes emerge as I reflect on my journey: learning, healing, and responding. I'll try to summarize my story through those three qualities of leadership.

## LEADERS MUST BE LEARNERS

I grew up in St. Catharines, Ontario, the fourth of five children and the only adopted child in our clan. My birth mother, Susie Schellenberg, was the youngest sister of my adopting mother, Tina. Susie was the first to give me an honest education about my origins. It's repugnant to learn that you began in trauma, unwanted, a crisis conception. In 1959 there were no legal abortion options in Canada, and Susie told me of her pleading before doctors and of her own crude avenues; she remembered making four unsuccessful attempts to end her pregnancy. It all left her desperately lonely and waiting to give birth at a Salvation Army home for unwed mothers in Hamilton, Ontario. I imagined that some angel in that place prayed over me...but Susie couldn't recall if anyone had. Susie struggled as a single mother, without government cheques or any social helps. She'd go off to hairdressing classes, leaving bottles in my crib, hoping I'd figure out how to feed myself. When I was two years old, she took me to an adoption agency and admitted she couldn't handle it anymore; I became a ward of the state.

Somebody *was* praying...Susie's older sister, Tina. Tina has told me that after a night on her knees, she knew she was to step forward to adopt me. Her doctor and her lawyer told her that her husband, Henry, did not have the temperament to add another child to their family, and they advised against the adoption. But she pressed on, and I had the good fortune of being placed in a somewhat open family adoption in a Christian home.

There were many problems. Learning that I was an unwanted mistake became a curse the devil wrapped deeply into every year of my young life. Many nights I cried myself to sleep, thinking it couldn't always be this way, and I dreamed of being an adult. When I turned 17, my dreams were dashed. I was in grade 12 when my conservative Mennonite father told me that going to university for a journalism degree as I'd intended was simply not going to happen. "The only career you need is to go to Bible school, marry a farmer and learn to be a good submissive wife" was Dad's exacting advice for me.

Dad handed me a brochure on Winkler Bible Institute (WBI) and told me that was where I would be going right after my pending grade 12 graduation. Back then in 1976 an Ontario student had to complete grade 13 to enrol in university, and I remember being stunned that the door was closed for me. I can clearly remember sitting on my bed with its white knit bedspread, looking out the window of my corner room and thinking I was doomed. Sure, I wanted to leave my restrictive home and move out—it was definitely a goal on my horizon—but I hadn't expected to have my choices in how and when I did that curtailed. There are always consequences to conflict, and the conflicts in our Christian home were now resulting in a parting of ways.

My summers in my high school years had always included working at a Bible camp, something Mom modelled for us through many summers of being a camp cook, and I took my turns being a lifeguard at various camps. So it was that we made a family plan that I would work as a lifeguard at the Winkler Bible Camp for the summer of 1977 and then begin school in the local Mennonite Brethren Bible school, WBI, in September.

The morning after my grade 12 graduation from Eden Christian High School, Mom and Dad packed me with them into a car and trailer unit and headed out on a 2,260 kilometre road trip of exile. I was angry and sullen the entire way, and when we reached Winkler, a small prairie town of approximately 3,000, we agreed that I would be dropped off at a phone booth across from the Dairy Queen restaurant. Mom and Dad had declared some terms: they would pay all my educational expenses and room and board for two years, and I would have to find any spending money on my own. My part of the bargain was that for the next year, I was not to contact home or any of my friends back in St. Catharines. Twelve months of forced separation.

I was shocked and spitting mad at Mom and Dad's terms. I don't remember their exact words, but the message was clear: "We need a break from you; we need to heal, and you need to figure yourself out. Goodbye." I was 17 and very angry at my parents.

I remember standing there, watching Mom and Dad's trailer head down the highway and weighing my options. I was in no spiritual condition to spend the summer at a Bible camp as a leader. I had been blessed by terrific Sunday school and girls' club teachers, a great youth pastor and 12 years of Christian primary and secondary education in excellent schools, but I was at a moment in life where I felt utterly unloved because of conflicts with Mom and Dad. A few months earlier I had concluded that "if" there was a God, this God certainly didn't love me. I was heading into the summer of the agnostic.

As I stood alone after that drop-off in Winkler, I thought about catching a Greyhound bus to Winnipeg and just living on the streets until I figured something out, but I didn't have enough cash to pay the bus fare. I had enough for the phone, so I reluctantly phoned the Bible camp and announced my arrival and location and asked for a ride out to camp.

Salvation happened at Winkler Bible Camp, but learning happened also—learning just how much difference loving, welcoming and selfless leaders can make in the lives of those who follow them. I arrived at Winkler Bible Camp a non-Christian, an angry teen who had left my childhood commitment to God over the anger I felt at being unloved at home. No one at camp knew my backstory; I was literally a strange girl who had arrived on the Manitoba prairie from Ontario, and the staff simply loved me.

There are too many names to mention them all, but every summer day off, either the camp cook, Audrey Dyck, or the camp directors, Ted and Mary Goossen, or a senior staffer took me to their home. It didn't matter to them that I wasn't attending camp chapels or morning devotionals; I was a lonely teen who needed loving. By the end of the summer, the staff examples of selfless service for others and open welcome to all had melted my objection to God's love. I was in, all in, and over the campfire one late August night, I did the camp's spiritual ritual, throwing a stick in the fire to symbolize that I was coming home to Jesus' salvation. The camp song at the fireside ceremony that night reflected my heart's desire: "This little light of mine, I'm going to let it shine."

When my classes at WBI began, I started a school newspaper. Classes were demanding on basic Bible content, and the professors had endless time for coaching us, including my Old Testament professor, John H. Goossen. At the end of my second year and just prior to graduation, Professor Goossen said, "Lorna, you've got such determination in your step; what is it you want to do with your life after WBI?"

I told Dr. Goossen I wanted to be a news reporter and a broadcaster, but I didn't know how to start that path because I felt my parents had closed the door to a university education. He smiled and wrote a name and phone number down on a piece of paper and said, "Tell this man I am sending you, and go see him."

Networking, as all leaders know, is invaluable, and we need to do it for the young people in our lives. I would later learn that the networking Professor Goossen was on the board of directors of Radio Southern Manitoba and Golden West Broadcasting, and he had given me the name of Elmer Hildebrand, the manager of the Radio Southern Manitoba consortium of radio stations. In 1977, with nothing more than a Bible school diploma to my credit, Elmer Hildebrand hired me right after graduation as the first female news announcer of their network. On the first day of work I was assigned to a four-person airplane with the most experienced agriculture reporter in Manitoba, and we took to the skies for a sweeping aerial view and a broadcast on the devastating Red River flood of the spring of 1977. With the kindness of God, my career in journalism had taken off.

I have been gifted with the vocal pitch of a broadcaster's voice. My family was the first to tell me this when one day in the summer after grade 8 I came home in tears over a trauma at the bank. The bank teller had looked at my pageboy haircut and flat chest and decided I was not a girl and not entitled to be holding my bankbook. My dad told me then, "Lorna, it's not your haircut that made her doubt you were a girl. It's your voice. Your voice is different than everyone else's, and God is going to use it some day for something special." That word of hope to my crushed self-esteem was a word of blessing, and it has never left me.

My father was a hardworking harsh man who didn't do well at giving me spoken blessings, but his words about God wanting to use my voice were a blessing that Dad and I talked over, even when he was over 80 years old. I am glad Dad knew he was a critical shaper of my career choice because he spoke that word of blessing to me. God makes a way for truth on our identity, even when we have to learn it in usual ways. That early word from my dad has always stayed with me, especially when I felt stretched beyond capacity to move into speaking publically about Christianity.

As I settled into radio reporting, I earned a basic community college diploma in journalism and began tackling interviewing and writing with gusto. Then it came time to slug out the 4 a.m. shifts, weekends, and late night beats in the larger city market of Winnipeg. I was a new wife and alarmed at the hours. I tucked my tail and played chicken and for the next four years took a government clerical role of nine to five.

When we moved to Brandon, Manitoba, for my husband's teaching certificate education, I was home in my apartment waiting for a clerical transfer with my government work. I was praying, on my knees, serious about my devotional life and my future, and I felt the Holy Spirit tell me to go apply to the local TV station in Brandon, Manitoba, for work. I called CKX Television and landed a job interview, and I began my first stint in television news. It was also the first job where I began to exercise my spiritual muscles for witness in the workplace.

The first step in learning is bowing down to God (Proverbs 1:7, MSG). Bowing down to God has been a wonderful lifelong learning process for me. The focus of that experience comes for me most mornings, when I intentionally set myself aside for 30 to 60 minutes of quiet time with God. I anchor this time in Bible reading and have often done this through the experience of reading through the Bible in a year (most recently doing it with an audio version). Sometimes I have instead used my daily Bible time to follow a Bible study manual, from Beth Moore or any variety of Christian authors. Most days I write out my prayers and thoughts with God in a few hundred words that I capture in one of my journals, a colourful collection of handwritten books that have now become a stunning record of God's faithfulness to me. Bowing down to God, or as other Bible translations put it, "the fear of God," is a lifelong discipline. I do believe that obedience to God is the critical path to gaining wisdom.

But I always hankered for that university degree, and in 2009 I was likely the happiest graduate on the stage of Tyndale University College when I finally received my bachelor of religious education, a degree I chipped away at on Thursday evenings over three years. In 2011, I started working on a master of evangelism and leadership degree at Wheaton

Graduate School. Wheaton is a suburb on the west side of Chicago that I came to call my "shire," and I enjoyed retreating twice a year to its idyllic culture, like a postcard out of the 1950s. It's a quaint academic town that just breathes rest and renewal from every white picket fence.

The studies were rigorous, and each course required about 600 pages of advance reading and book-report writing. Professors Rick Richardson, Beth Severson and Lon Allison (all good friends of mine) had designed this unique degree to help students understand the theology of evangelism and the gospel and how to communicate it better. We studied apologetics and culture, designed debate around hot social issues and explored how to respond to tough questions people have about the existence of God. My four years of study at the Wheaton seminary plunged me deep into evaluating what it is that makes mission work effective, and it led me on some fascinating field trips.

My biggest takeaway from my formative years at Wheaton has been that there is no substitute for simply obeying the command of Christ to "Go." Whether at a festival, our kitchen table or our workplace, we simply have to speak to people about what we know about Jesus and invite them to Christ's salvation. It's not rocket science; it's the gospel.

Learning how to listen for God's voice through the Holy Spirit—be it through course study, daily devotions, mentoring relationships or in the humility and discipline of cleaning the house after Vern and the children—and learning how to respond to God have always been the lifeblood of my leadership.

## LEADERS MUST BE HEALERS

I wince at the reality of how easy it is for me to hurt people emotionally. I've wired my world to be fast, communicative and influential, and occasionally someone has had the nerve to tell me what it meant to be run over by my style. Sometimes our own wounds are what cause us to hurt others.

We had only been married a few weeks when my husband, Vern, said to me, "I don't know what all happened in your childhood, but you don't take criticism very well. I'm not going to criticize you." That was terrific news, and for me it worked wonderfully for the first ten years of our marriage.

Some background here now on Vern, who has been a terrific husband for 35 years, a healing, stabilizing and inspiring force in my life. Vern is a financial planner and runs his own business, Stewardsway Financial. Vern is a smart, analytical man who has trained and worked as a high school teacher and tackled a few other ventures. I met Vern at WBI, and neither Vern nor I had seriously dated or kissed anyone prior to meeting each other. Vern has seven siblings and is from a wonderful Manitoba farming family. One night in 1978 during the harvest season after the work had stopped, Vern and I took a walk down his family's beautiful country lane under the stars and silence, and I reviewed with him all I had observed on this my first day out with his family on a farming workday. I told him I could never marry into his clan. They were all just too nice, and I wasn't sweet enough to fit in. He laughed and drew me close and under the star-filled prairie night said, "If I had a ring right now, I'd give to it you." We dated 18 months, committed our lives to God under the invitation of Colossians 3:12–17, and have been happily married ever since. And his family are still wonderful people. (Watch the YouTube video "The Margaret Dueck Story" at https://www.youtube.com/watch?v=YSG0r3V7AB0 for a glimpse into the quality in this clan.)

Vern was not the first in my life to notice I needed healing for a childhood that had been marked by abuse. At the ten-year anniversary of our marriage, he asked that we go to marriage counselling. At the time we were living in Steinbach, Manitoba, where Vern had opened a restaurant and pizza wholesaling business, and we were attending the Mennonite Brethren Church. It was 1989. Our son, Adam, was three years old, and Elise was just over a year old. I declined Vern's suggestion, rather indignant about putting any personal material before a counsellor, and thought I was managing everything just fine.

A short time later, my ability to hurt others reared its ugly head, and when little Adam couldn't get his mitten on, I smacked him across the head. I was horrified at myself and told Vern I would take up his invitation to go for counselling. The counsellor, Dan Thiessen, was a friend of Vern's, a pastoral intern at our church and a student in Providence College's program in Christian counselling.

In the first visit Dan pushed a piece of paper toward me and asked me to write down a dominant memory for each year of my life. I pushed the paper back at him and said something like "No. Been there, done that, don't need to." I recall Vern gently stroking my back and saying "Trust me; you need this." Here was a man who had for ten years been my Prince

Charming. He had never raised his voice at me. He showered me with kindness and generosity, encouraged my gifting and passions, and he was asking me to dig up my painful memories. "Trust me," Vern asked, and I knew I could trust Vern deeply to be there if I fell apart over where I needed to go.

Trust is essential for healing. More than the reliability of Vern, I was coming to discover the deep trustworthiness of God for healing. It was in this season of being a young mother, immersed into the full-time care of two toddlers, that I began to learn how to have a daily quiet time with my Bible and journal. I used this time to begin to go through my memories and struggle to turn to God for a deeper inner healing of my own attitudes and fears. Psalm 139:13–16 drew me like a magnet:

*For you formed my inward parts; you knitted me together in my mother's womb. I praise you, for I am fearfully and wonderfully made. Wonderful are your works; my soul knows it very well. My frame was not hidden from you, when I was being made in secret, intricately woven in the depths of the earth. Your eyes saw my unformed substance; in your book were written, every one of them, the days that were formed for me, when as yet there was none of them.*

This passage from Psalm 139 put God into the dark issues that dogged me about my own worth. It gave me the welcome to see my origin as coming not from the narrative of "I was a mistake" but from the intentions of God, and it pulled me deeper toward finding my roots in God. I was not an accident; I was the work of God, and that truth deeply affected me.

In that season of inner healing, when I was between 28 and 32 years old, I received supportive healing from the family of God. I recall many honest and accepting conversations when at least 30 different friends, patient and trusted intercessors, counsellors and pastors, came to me one or two at a time, always at a time I needed it, and laid hands on me and prayed for me on my meandering journey to emotional healing and a deeper walk with God. I was often an open book with a complicated plot line en route to the Saviour. Always there was a way station in the presence of a loving Christian to whom I could take my expressive temperament for healing. Other sisters in Christ were available to help me make sense of my mistakes, hurts and wounds and to help me discover a resting ground at the foot of the cross of Jesus. To this day many of these women remain close friends from their gift of communicating the reality that Jesus gave His life so I could be repaired through forgiveness and love.

I look back on living 20 years and more with my friends Barb, Deborah and Sandy, Christine and others, healers with Christ, and smile with deep gratitude that a leader's journey seldom needs to be a lonely one. These are women who have always been available to me. We have worked hard at protecting time and communication with each other, dedicating time to friendship and scheduling to make it happen. None of the relationships survives "naturally"; we all work at pursuing each other.

Because this is a book on leadership, I've needed to describe my own inner healing to explain that character is at the core of how we lead. Character comes from our identity, who we are in our conscious and subconscious, and keeping our identity shaped by Christ is a spiritual discipline helped much by loving friendships and our personal devotion to the Bible.

The resurrection of Christ is victory over everything in our lives and on earth that is broken. I look forward to the heaven that Christ is creating for the end of our lives, and meanwhile the heaven that Jesus invites us to co-create on earth through our walk with Him is deeply satisfying to me. Since I experienced a new life in Christ, this focus on God in our personal life and God in our global life became two constants that shaped the media stories of God that I was being led into. I wanted to find the stories that showed how God got engaged in healing people and the world and to report them as encouragement and evidence for others.

## LEADERS MUST BE RESPONDERS

A. W. Tozer wrote, "[Great saints] differed from the average person in that when they felt the inward longing, they *did something about it.* They acquired the lifelong habit of spiritual response."[2]

I am always surprised at the beauty of the local church. God speaks to me each Sunday I show up, refreshing, encouraging and equipping me, and while many Sundays I've felt a temptation to stay away— sometimes just lazy, sometimes to fuel my need for quiet and introspection—I'm always glad after I've gone to church. Vern and I have attended six congregations

---

[2] A. W. Tozer, *Tozer on the Almighty God: A 365-Day Devotional* (Chicago: Moody Publishers, 2015), 5.

through our 35 years together. We've ranged from Mennonite Brethren to charismatic, and we've had our longest home in the Christian and Missionary Alliance in Burlington, Ontario, these past 20 years. Our children were just entering their teens when we settled here, attracted because the Alliance was a church family that bustled with outreach and evangelism. But in our younger years we stuck closer to our Mennonite roots, and at one of the mission services at Steinbach Mennonite Brethren Church, Rev. Dave Currie was used of God to inspire us both to be willing to give our lives for full-time mission work. We both went forward together for an altar call of dedication at the front of the church that Sunday evening mission service when Dave was preaching. Vern and I had a sense that God was inviting us to combine work and ministry, but we had no clear game plan at all.

Sometime later, we got that inner nudge that it was the right time to sell Vern's restaurant and frozen pizza manufacturing operation. This business had been a great adventure for Vern, a job well done, and the sale went through quickly, giving us financial flexibility and plenty of time to ponder if Vern should return to teaching high school or if we should venture elsewhere. A short time later, I was tucking away the Christmas tree as we entered the new year of 1994, and Vern said to me, "Well, if we're serious about being available for God, we should sell the house too."

Vern and I have quite opposite temperaments, and he is always the cautious one, so I couldn't believe the challenge he was placing before me. We had just 936 square feet in the first home we owned, but I loved every inch of that possession. I knew he was right, and the house went up for sale.

We trooped off to an older mentor couple in church who we thought had navigated much of being available for God, and they took us in for long walks and prayer times, helping us see Hebrews 11:8 as a life verse for that season: "By faith Abraham obeyed when he was called to go out to a place that he was to receive as an inheritance. And he went out, not knowing where he was going."

All this change and this call to a new life for mission happened in the same church where the all-male elders' board asked me to stop teaching a women's Sunday school class because my teaching style through the Psalms was getting "too personal." Devastated at that judgment and being dismissed from leadership, I reached out to a book mentor I had at the time, Anne Ortlund. I had been modelling my teaching style on Anne's *Love One Another* book, and in 1989 when the Internet was not yet commonplace, I wrote and mailed Anne a tear-filled letter about how a local church could spurn a volunteer; what could I possibly have done wrong?

Having never met me, Anne picked up the phone and told me my method was right, but I should be patient with my church and just go quiet for a season and let the Lord sort it out, to receive it as God's discipline for a season. That call from a leader, who took time from her busy life to care for me without knowing me or my dreams, still reminds me of how important it is for leaders to slow down and encourage others. A leader's words have enormous weight to build up or tear down.

Two more times in the course of that year in that Mennonite community church I would be rebuked by church members for using my own words unwisely, and it devastated me. At the time I had no idea that I would find myself on live national television explaining the gospel to tens of thousands of people, in live conversations where a redo was just not possible. Serving in the local church was part of my training ground of knowing how to hold my tongue and use my words wisely and with discretion, something I still struggle with.

So it was that while I was stirring spaghetti in our Steinbach home kitchen one day in June 1994, the phone rang with a call from Reverend David Mainse. Networking had been going on behind the scenes with two good friends, Karen Pascal and Brian Stiller, and I had recently met Rev. Mainse through this. When listening to Rev. Mainse preach in Winnipeg one night after that networking visit, I had decided that if he ever needed any help, I'd be happy to assist him. Now only a few weeks later, David was calling to ask me to bring my family to his 100 Huntley Street studio in Burlington and spend a week on air with his national daily TV ministry to audition for a full-time on-air position as his co-host.

Vern and I knew we had to check it out. Rev. David Mainse was taking the filling of this position of his on-air co-host role in deep prayer, and discerning a family fit, not just an individual fit, was all part of the climate he set in hiring key roles. Norma Jean Mainse has a remarkable gift of hospitality and decked out her farm home dining room with an elegant dinner to welcome us. I remember the children looking at me, wondering which fork they should pick up, since the cutlery extended as long as their elbows. It was just the beginning of a loving, caring relationship with the Mainse family for the eight years we would work together.

At the close of the audition week, David offered me the job at a four-day-a-week hire. I was overwhelmed, but Vern thought it was a perfect fit. I asked Vern to drop me off at a quiet park where I could pray, and he knowingly went off to find us a place to live. Four work days a week...I knew my own clock, and I knew I needed a three-day weekend to pull my own homemaking together. Our children were in going into grade 2 and grade 4, and I had never worked full time away from them but had rather been juggling a home office, writing freelance stories for radio and print markets. The four-day-a-week offer was the clincher for me. We moved with 23 days' notice, and I went from a quiet basement office in my home, wearing sweatpants or whatever, to national television, where what I wore really mattered. It wasn't an easy move from small Manitoba prairie town to big Ontario city. Vern would have to find work in province he'd never lived in, the kids would need a new school, the cost of living was nearly double what we were used to, and we arrived in Burlington without a friend in sight.

There are so many stories I could tell about this season of responding, but perhaps I could sum it up with this principle: the Holy Spirit is actively involved in the work of calling individuals to change their patterns and preferences and take up a task that God is inviting them to. God has always worked with and through people, and it may surprise you that God chooses to work with you. Say yes to the inner prompts the Holy Spirit lays on your heart, and notice when peace and harmony come from decisions of sacrifice and surrender. Drink deeply from the well of worship and the Word of God during seasons of calling and transition; they are critical times of personal and professional development.

Working with the Mainse family and their dedicated, talented staff of producers, technicians, administrators and prayer partners of the Crossroads Family of Ministries remains a deeply formative time of my leadership. I felt completely inadequate to be among them, but two things kept me on the job in the first tentative year: public need, and David's encouragement. I felt I was a cheesy TV host, and yet, when we put up a telephone number on the screen for prayer, over 1,000 people a day would call that line for prayer as a result of the broadcast. That is still a dynamic that occurs from the *100 Huntley Street* broadcast, and it's a humbling reminder that we live in a country where people are desperate for God's help. David modelled that this was a task to steward with a daily dependence on God, and in the first days of work I stumbled across my new boss lying prostrate before God at the Crossroads chapel altar in the early morning. His daily routine I would learn was to arrive at the office well before anyone else and spend from 5 a.m. to 7 a.m. with God.

Leaders pass on much through their actions, and David was a mentor on the run to me, rarely shutting the door to an idea I had, always quick to facilitate my creativity and curiosity, always putting me in the deep end of an event and creating conditions for my leadership to flourish. He stood like a rock on things he wouldn't budge over, like every episode needing a salvation testimony, and I soon adapted my journalistic interests to asking the tough questions about how people came to understand Jesus as Saviour and how they knew that God was present in their lives. My penchant for wanting to work journalistically with news events for a Christian response was new for *100 Huntley Street*, and David loved it.

Soon he challenged me to produce a half hour on *Huntley*'s Thursday broadcasts with a show dedicated to that focus. We called the experiment *Listen Up*, the intent being to listen to the world and then look up to God for perspective. "Oh, and fundraise for the costs of that half hour," said David in what appeared to be a rather casual remark to me during the early planning of *Listen Up*. In reality, this toss into the fundraising world became critical to my leadership development. Fundraising is like a muscle that must be exercised to be strong, and resource raising is a fundamental part of leadership. By now I too had become accustomed to lying on the floor with my face buried in the carpet, asking God for the strength to do what was needed, and fundraising had its start in that posture and still finds strength in that stance. When leaders are asked to fundraise, our job is to partner with the Holy Spirit to help others be blessed by God's call for their resources.

I again experienced a deeper level of inner healing working with the Pentecostal team at 100 Huntley Street, and I loved the adventures of reporting that took me to places and people like Sierra Leone's civil war victims, India's need for medical missions, addiction and abuse recovery in remote Shesatshiu, Labrador, and many other news gathering locations in Canada.

But after eight years, I was watching our family dynamics shift and was feeling uncomfortable about never being home for breakfast with my children, and I was in a season of prayer over that discontent. Adam and Elise were entering their teen years, and I was not happy with the stress I was seeing in their lives, and my own. David's sons were stepping into their own leadership at the broadcast, and so I headed off to a personal prayer retreat wondering if it might be the season I was being called back home to be a full-time mom. As my van hit the highway en route to the quiet Catholic convent I would retreat to for occasional days of prayer, I heard the Holy Spirit speak to my heart, "Use this time to write resignation letters."

I left the job I deeply loved in mid-June 2006 and came home. My young teens were alarmed that I had far too much time to focus on them, but I remember it as a sweet season of beautiful renewal and refreshing for me. Summer unfolded, and I filled the weeks as a watchful mom over kids and the entertaining that comes with their friends and activities. As the kids headed off to school in the fall of that year, silence descended as I sat in my devotional chair, a special place that has always been my designated chapel with my books, coffee, and window to our back garden. I watched the leaves fall off the trees and the greenery go dormant, and I embraced the word-picture before me, clearly understanding that this was my season to let God renew me for a fruitfulness that would return. For now, I was to be quiet.

It was in these days that Dr. Lon Allison, director of the Billy Graham Center at Wheaton College, phoned me to invite me to join a global mentoring group of younger evangelists. I had taken a course with Lon when I was enrolled in the Arrow Leadership Program, and he had remembered my passion for media and felt it would be a good fit for his new group. I thanked him but told him I was unemployed, out of media and in a season of just resting in God. "No problem," said Lon, "we still need you...just pray about it and let me know."

Again, God was using another leader to encourage me that there was an evangelism gifting in me, and in God's time it would be nurtured. Lon's group has come to be called the Star Fellowship, based on Daniel 4:11, and we've become a tight group of leaders who are in our twelfth year of gathering for an annual four-day retreat and who pepper each other with prayer support throughout the year.

After about eight months of being unemployed, I was asked by David Mainse to come in to meet with him. I was happy to go see my old boss and catch up on things. But David had an agenda, and he shared that he didn't like the idea of me sitting idle. "You have a calling on your life for broadcast evangelism, and God is not finished with you on this," said David. He proposed that I take the idea of *Listen Up* and craft it into an independent charity and just see what God would do with the efforts. David suggested that I freely use the resources of a Crossroads consultant and former board chair, Marten Mol, to help create the charity, and he said that Crossroads would give me a year of airtime on Thursday mornings, free office space and all the support I might require. That was a lot to think about.

I wasn't too keen on the prospect. The daunting task of fundraising and administration weighed heavily on me. Within days, an unexpected phone call came from an editor at the *Globe and Mail* newspaper. Editor Patrick Martin, a highly respected shaper of Canadian culture, had been fielding occasional freelance pieces from stories I had adapted for the *Globe* from content that I worked on at *100 Huntley Street* or *Listen Up*. Patrick was now asking me to be a regular monthly columnist at Canada's most-read national newspaper; a million readers every day look through its pages.

Lon, David and Patrick were all inviting me to get out of my dormant stage. I felt like I was facing the turning of the page: stay home and bake cookies, or answer the invitation to be a public voice on Christianity. Vern had one of those wise moments he is so prone to and gently said, "I think what the kids need most is to see a mother who obeys God."

The following summer I took this fledgling project of an independent *Listen Up* TV program to the Banff World Media Festival, thinking I would work on selling the concept to a broadcaster rather than creating a charitable model for it. The market realities showed me that whoever owns the broadcast owns the content, and the only way to ensure that stories remained Christ-centred would be to own them. It was a key tipping point in creating Media Voice Generation, a media charity that would have a weekly half-hour television show as its flagship effort. Like a scared Gideon who needed to be told "be strong, take courage," I put out a few fleeces so I would know I was walking in God's will. I needed a team of three to launch a new board of directors, and I wanted a generous line of financial credit from a donor before I could commit.

Dr. Franklin Pyles was the chairman of the Christian Missionary Alliance denomination, and he had frequently dropped me notes of encouragement about my writing. My first fleece was that if Franklin would say yes to leading our board, I'd move forward, and Franklin did indeed say yes. Little did I know how his leadership of 400 Canadian churches would bring management and practical skills that would see our efforts through many harrowing and often self-inflicted challenges.

Next, I approached the Honourable Preston Manning and his wife, Sandra, to serve as vice-chairs of this new charity, and remarkably this busy couple agreed. Preston Manning's father, Ernest, had come to Christ through the radio preaching of "Bible Bill Aberhart," and I was hoping that the Manning clan still valued media witness. I certainly wasn't disappointed; Franklin Pyles and Preston and Sandra Manning remain close friends to me and the work to this day.

Finally, there was that heavy issue of money. How would I fund a charity? I love leadership biographies, and our consultant Marten Mol had given me a collection of stories of how Dutch entrepreneurs had established their businesses in Ontario. One story sparkled to me; it was about two brothers who ached to have a bakery but couldn't find a line of credit to get their dreams off the ground. Harry Voortman was one of those Dutch baking brothers, and now he had a factory not far from my home that employed hundreds of bakers, and his famous Voortman cookies could be bought around the world. Harry and his wife, Anne, were generous supporters of *100 Huntley Street*, and I didn't want to distract their donations. Rather, I asked if they would be my backup guarantors for a line of credit as I started a new charity, Media Voice Generation. I was quaking in fear as I sat down to ask, completely inexperienced in such negotiations.

Harry listened to the vision I had to engage news and current events with a bridge to Christ. He asked me, "How much do you think you need?" I said that I thought I would need a line of credit for $500,000. He smiled and said, "I was thinking this should require a million dollar line of credit."

So thus began one of the most vital links to launching a new public media witness in Christianity. Donors are the team, and by the grace of God about 400 donors a year contributed faithfully to meet the annual budget but never quite fast enough to build the reserves that networks and broadcast suppliers require. We dipped in and out of Harry's line of credit, always ending in the positive by our year-end, our team of 400 always filling the need to bring us into a balanced budget during each 12 month fiscal cycle. It's been a remarkable experience of depending on the generosity of God to move the generosity of His people.

My 50th year, 2010, was a pivotal time for responding to the Holy Spirit's moving in my life. I've dug out my personal journals for some reminders of that, and I smiled to see that I chose Hebrews 12 as my focus for that year. It's a Bible chapter that challenges us to "run with perseverance the race marked out for us, fixing our eyes on Jesus" (Hebrews 12:1-2, NIV). It teaches us the importance of responding to God's discipline in our life and invites us to live in the absolute welcome of God and respond to the God who speaks to us. Little did I know how many decisions lay ahead where I would need to sink deeply into the advice of Hebrews 12.

As 2010 began, I was painstakingly putting together a documentary looking at the rescue of an Inuit boy, Jupi Angootealuk, who had been stranded on an ice floe with three polar bears in November 2009. Remarkably the story uncovered not only Jupi's rescue but a movement of Inuit men involved in spiritual rescue for the souls of their families in Canada's far north. Within weeks I was off again with our excellent cameraman and editor Moussa Faddoul to report from the front lines of the Haitian earthquake that killed over 160,000 people and left more than 300,000 homeless—staggering numbers on suffering. We were there to record how CBM Canada was responding to the disabilities the earthquake inflicted and to help answer the age-old question "If there is a God...why?" Our files at Media Voice Generation are full of Christians responding with the love and care of God, stories that have always made people ask "Where is God?" God is active when people step out in love and faith to care for the suffering. We documented God's love through people's helping hands in the 2004 Asian tsunami that killed 280,000, the crisis of Hurricane Katrina, the intervention into human trafficking, the care for victims of the war launched by ISIS and many other stories.

But now it was our turn to head out into the impossible. Another learning trip to the Banff World Media Festival, this time in spring 2010, had left a deep calling in me that our media charity was called to aim its voice at secular-minded Canadians. I had what I describe as a "holy unrest" that we could do better in public witness than what we were doing tucked safely as renters from the larger Crossroads Christian Communications. Amid these wonderings, a management friend at the Canadian Broadcasting Corporation said to me, "You need to bring your production work here, into Toronto; this is where you should make TV." So it was that a few weeks after returning from Banff, I was walking in Toronto's entertainment and media district when I spotted the old Wesley building at John and Queen Street and was stunned by the lineup around its block. In the early 1900s, the Wesley building (named for famed British evangelist John Wesley) was the centre for the publication of Christian literature and Bibles. After it was sold in the 1970s the building housed a TV station and production facilities for Bell Globe Media, producing media for millions of minds, but none of that media was faith based.

On this day in 2010 as I walked the nearby street, the Wesley building was jammed with kids camped out around it. I saw scores of teenagers waiting for Much Music wristbands so they could attend an exciting awards broadcast. The roof of the old building was full of satellite dishes, and the picture of communication power was unmistakable. I had an encounter with the Holy Spirit on that walk, and I heard an audible invitation from God that this was the neighbourhood to be working in, that God was inviting me to create a media home for God's work in downtown Toronto. Our board of directors was meeting shortly, and I put together a vision pitch to move out of our comfortable, safe ministry office in the Crossroads Centre in Burlington and attempt to lease a new office in Toronto's entertainment and media district.

We began with the Canadian Broadcasting Corporation, which received just over one billion dollars a year from government tax funding to create media. The CBC building covered an entire block near the Wesley building, and its ten floors were a prestigious address known for influence and power. Within 15 minutes of discussion, our board unanimously said, "Go." We spent the next nine months knocking on doors at the CBC, being refused and ignored, but we persisted and continued with prayer walks around and in the building. A charity is only as strong as its board of directors, and eventually it was a strategic phone call from one of our board members, Preston Manning, to Hubert LaCroix, then president of the CBC, that made the deal come into play. The specifics were daunting: a five-year lease at a 70 percent increase over our current operations and conditions that included the golden handcuffs that we had to use CBC technical crew to produce our material.

As always, Christians would have to own the product; there would be no money available from any of secular media operations to produce Christian content. We had a thirty-day window before us in which to decide before CBC would withdraw the offer. Our plan for this move would be to double the amount of media we were putting out and increase Christian witness in a secular market, but the mountain before us was huge.

We held our next board meeting in a boardroom at the CBC, thinking we'd pray for discernment from within the territory we wanted. In its 11-year history, our board has always moved in unity, prayed and made bold decisions that kept our focus on reaching non-Christian people. A five-year lease would add $1.8 million to our funding needs. Our fearless director of fundraising and strategy, Jeff Groenewald, put together a 30-day campaign to ask 12 families in Canada to commit portions to cover that $1.8 million in a five-year commitment to our lease. Thirty days later, signed commitments were in, and the board voted that we should go ahead and accept the CBC lease and begin construction on a main-floor office in the heart of Canada's media industry. God's team had expanded and stepped up to create a new home for Media Voice Generation. We hired a trusted branding expert to help us wrestle out what the new one should look like and rebranded our TV work as "Context with Lorna Dueck."

In any venture of responding to God, it's good to stay anchored in the Bible. I love Luke 8, a chapter that teaches that God's work is like a generous sowing of seeds. It's a parable where the word "broadcaster" originates, and I've been challenged to model my life as one who generously broadcasts the seeds of God on all sorts of ground. Many good people have been a part of this journey, and it's a joy to continue to tell the stories of how God pursues people with love and salvation, just like He pursued me.

As 2016 dawned, a new leadership season began in both my life and the work of Context TV and Media Voice Generation. In my devotional on January 1, 2016, I prayed for a word to focus my efforts on for the year. In my journal I recorded the word "fruitful." I wanted 2016 to be a year of being fruitful for God, but I knew some tasks in my life would be pruned for new fruit to develop.

Context TV was growing as we had planned for. In 2014 I had drawn our board of directors together to initiate the discussion of succession planning. This was a needed step in exploring how we could transition the media work into a broader base with a full-time president, who would set strategy and guide our charity leadership. Jeff Groenewald, a trusted friend and a fine leader for God's purposes, was selected to be the new president at Context TV. Other leaders sowed into Jeff's life while he was in university, and there he answered a call from God to be a "world changer." Jeff's had a lifetime career in serving God with Power to Change and Opportunity International, and he quickly set higher targets for Context TV, expanding our media ministry into a team that produced daily digital media deliveries, not just a weekly TV broadcast. By spring 2016, this new growth in Context's media work had tripled online audiences, and I had a growing sense that Context was simply not large enough to handle the new realities.

In May 2016, I was walking Parliament Hill in prayer. It was a quiet few moments following a morning at the National Prayer Breakfast. Again I was wrestling with what I sensed was the Holy Spirit telling me that Context needed to grow. That afternoon at a ministry function in Ottawa, Melissa McEachern, executive producer of *100 Huntley Street*, approached me, and we exchanged stories of our media challenges. Melissa is a sharp young leader, a good listener and a personal friend. I soon knew that our conversation was getting deep on our mutual passion for Christian media. Mid-sentence, Melissa stopped and looked deep into me and asked if I would consider letting my name be submitted to the Crossroads board of directors search committee that was looking for a new leader to run a historic Canadian media ministry.

That board process of interviews and diligence has resulted in a wonderful return for me to the broadcast ministry that taught me so much about the formation of a public voice for Christ. As CEO of Crossroads, YES TV and Tricord Media, there is much to lead.

David Mainse, the ministry founder and *100 Huntley Street* host for over 10,000 daily TV programs, now almost 80 years old, cried "happy tears" when told that I wanted to accept the board's invitation to become the leader of the ministry he continues to care for deeply. Before any of the staff or public knew this news, I drove out again to David and Norma Jean's home for one of her wonderful dinners, and we talked, laughed, cried and prayed together.

In my new leadership role, I am blessed to have a team of 120 staff, 100 volunteers and 20,000 donors now helping do the work of spreading the gospel through media. At Crossroads and YES TV, there is a thirty-five million dollar engine of donations and broadcast revenues that fuels this work. This team tackles a daily national evangelistic broadcast, *100 Huntley Street*; it answers hundreds of calls for prayer each day; and it ensures that Context TV's unique approach to secular viewers reaches out with the gospel to people not yet Christian. YES TV has three 24-hour TV stations that help spread the gospel 24 hours a day. I have a new leadership vision to be the kind of leader who passes media evangelism from one generation to a new generation coming up behind her. If we do not speak the gospel, we lose it.

When I began media work, I had a founding psalm that served to light the path before me, and it continues to guide me to this day:

*One generation shall commend your works to another, and shall declare your mighty acts. On the glorious splendor of your majesty, and on your wondrous works, I will meditate. They shall speak of the might of your awesome deeds, and I will declare your greatness. They shall pour forth the fame of your abundant goodness and shall sing aloud of your righteousness.* (Psalm 145:4–7)

---

Lorna Dueck has explored the intersection of journalism and Christianity for over 30 years. In 2016, she was appointed CEO of the Crossroads Global Media Group. Crossroads oversees the YES TV network, its faith and values media distributor Tricord Media, and *100 Huntley Street*, Canada's longest running daily TV talk show and prayer line ministry. For 11 years prior, Lorna was CEO at Media Voice Generation (MVG), a community-held Canadian charity that created the award-winning TV program *Context With Lorna Dueck*, which featured news analysis from a Christian perspective. Lorna is also a commentary writer on faith and public life in Canada's leading national newspaper, *The Globe and Mail*.

Lorna began her media career in radio with Golden West Broadcasting in Manitoba and began Christian TV work in 1994 as the co-host of *100 Huntley Street*. She completed a bachelor of religious education at Tyndale University College in Toronto, earned a master of arts in evangelism and leadership from Wheaton College, and has received honorary doctorate degrees from Trinity, Tyndale, and Briercrest universities. Lorna has been honoured with the Queen's Diamond Jubilee Medal for contributions to Canadian society.

Lorna and Vern live in Burlington, Ontario, have been married over three decades, and delight in the adventures of their grown son and daughter.

# *Starting*

## Over and Finishing Well

by Georgialee Lang

There's nothing like Vancouver in June: lush trees with whispering leaves and birds humming, all amid a blue sky gleaming in the sunlight. It was a perfect day for a drive, and I remember sitting in the back seat of a vehicle winding down a steep hill, expertly maneuvered by a blue-suited police officer. I was in a cruiser with my neck stretched toward the window as a foreboding brick and steel structure, built in 1912, came into view. It was my new home: Oakalla Prison for Women. The year was 1974.

Almost 40 years later, there was another car ride. This trip took me along the elegant Rideau Canal in Ottawa on a windy, drizzly day in autumn, the rain almost obscuring the tangerine, yellow and scarlet landscape that flanked the waterway. This time I peered through the foggy windows to see a magnificent art deco structure with massive gleaming golden doors. No, it wasn't the Land of Oz; I had arrived at the Supreme Court of Canada. I closed my umbrella and walked across the polished marble of the great hall to attend a private cocktail party at the invitation of Chief Justice Beverley McLachlin.

You may be thinking, how do you journey from a women's prison to the halls of the highest court in the land? There is only one way: through God's grace.

&#x2113;

I was a skinny redheaded kid with seven siblings, a father who toiled on the green chain at a mill and a stay-at-home mom who had emigrated from Holland to Canada. I wasn't smart or pretty; in fact, my oldest brother called me ugly. I knew early on that my insular parents could never introduce me to the world I observed from a distance. As a teenager in the '60s I longed for a poorboy sweater and a flowered miniskirt—what all the other girls wore. I dreamt of eating at McDonald's and fantasized about family trips to Disneyland. But I realized at a young age that this would never happen.

Our usual diet was porridge, Cheez Whiz sandwiches on stale bread, lots of baloney, and powdered milk. Mom made pancakes with flour and water that we gorged on. At night we could smell the sizzling steak that my parents would fry after we were all in bed. It was the cheapest cut of meat my dad could find and a treat reserved for them, and they certainly deserved it. But the most difficult deprivation was the absence of emotional intimacy with my parents. My parents were good people and worked hard, but there was a coldness to their manner. My heart ached for basic affection, like hugging and kissing, and expressions of love and pride. No doubt the psychological pain from feeling unloved contributed to my social insecurities.

My earliest memories are of the Nazarene Church in Coquitlam, where, at the age of two, I was lifted onto the podium and sang all three verses of "When the Roll Is Called Up Yonder, I'll Be There." When I was ten, the organist at a small Baptist church in New Westminster heard me sing and suggested to my mom that I take voice lessons. Mom liked the idea but certainly couldn't afford to pay two dollars per lesson. The organist agreed to teach me for free and did so for over eight years. I loved classical voice training and entered local singing competitions and music festivals, and I sang in church and with my high school orchestra.

I acted self-assured and confident when I performed, but beneath the facade I was anxious and insecure. I couldn't make friends, and I didn't know why. (And it was far too painful for me to delve into that mire.) Decades later, after therapy, I realized that I suffered from the dreaded curse of perfectionism: never feeling good enough, smart enough or pretty enough. As I moved through my teen years, these feelings only intensified.

I became increasingly isolated but was always able to put on a happy face. I also loved my journalism classes and wrote prodigiously for my school newspaper and the local community paper. At age 16, as an insecure teenager with a polished "front," I entered a pageant, Miss Teen British Columbia, and I came in second. You may wonder what prompted a teenager with low self-esteem to become a pageant contestant! I believe that I was desperate to be affirmed, to be recognized, to feel better about myself—but the "high" was short-lived.

I was the first person in my extended family to graduate from high school, and I was awarded two scholarships, one in journalism and the other in vocal performance. I was grateful, although I felt disappointed that my mom and dad didn't attend my high school graduation ceremony.

The day after graduation I slipped out of the house and moved into my own apartment, with not a word to my parents or siblings. Nobody seemed to notice. I had worked part-time since the age of 12 at a succession of jobs, including delivering newspapers, shelving books at the local library, working at a Dairy Queen, and processing X-rays for a dentist. I hadn't been a real part of my family since I was 14. My life was school, work and eating alone at fast food restaurants with a book or a *True Detective* magazine. (My dad regularly scoured the nearby city dump and brought home ice cream, bread, potato chips and, best of all, magazines with lurid headlines about rape and murder.) As I grew older, I rarely sat still long enough to dream about or imagine my future. Nobody mentioned college or university. It was a non-issue.

At age 18, I acquired my first full-time job as a dental assistant for a local dentist. Then, a college opened in New Westminster. Douglas College had a well-respected music department, so I moved back home and enrolled as a vocal performance major, thriving under the tutorship of two talented voice professors. My goal to be the best coloratura soprano drove me to obsessively vocalize, learn operatic and lieder repertoire and rehearse five hours every day. My professors told me I had a future in opera and should consider further training or an internship at one of the many small opera houses in Europe.

Instead, I fell in love with a young man who also attended the college. He was handsome, smart and from a good family. His father was an accountant. I was entranced by his *Leave It to Beaver* family life, so different from mine. His mother baked cinnamon buns! Rob was one of those lucky kids whose parents sent him to Europe between high school and college, his "gap year." When he returned he brought with him pictures of European cities and a hankering for heroin, a drug that was in great supply in one of his favourite cities, Amsterdam.

It was the early '70s, and we were the generation known for Timothy Leary's counterculture phrase "Turn on, tune in, drop out." I had already smoked marijuana and dropped LSD once, so why not try heroin? Rob and I became weekend "chippers," a term used to describe the first stage of addiction.

Eventually life became centred on the "needle"—no college, no singing, just existing, living in fleabag hotels on the mean streets of Vancouver and moving every few weeks to the next dive, each one a little worse than the last. Rob bought small quantities of drugs to sell, and I was immersed in a foggy haze. I was no longer anxious or insecure, and it didn't matter that I had no friends. I had finally escaped...to nowhere.

It was inevitable that living on the "low down" in Vancouver's sleaziest neighbourhood would not end well. Eventually Rob was arrested for trafficking heroin, and with a crash at the front door of our spartan apartment in Burnaby, the drug squad descended and found a cap of heroin under a blouse in my closet. I was arrested for possession.

Rob pleaded guilty and began serving his two-year-less-a-day prison sentence at the men's unit at Oakalla Prison while I awaited my legal fate. On my own, without a male protector, I crumbled and was sucked further into an ugly black hole. A local pimp pressured me to travel with him and two of his best girls to Kamloops. And I did.

I arrived in the dingy town of Kamloops and—by God's mercy—recoiled from the life he invited me to join. That night, I purposely overdosed on pills, ending up in police lock-up. I was flown by air ambulance from Kamloops to New Westminster, where I awoke in Royal Columbian Hospital. My face was bruised and battered. I wasn't sure why, but as I lay in bed resting, I realized that I had narrowly escaped a lifetime of addition and prostitution. I had just turned 20.

The early '70s in Canada was a time when judges eschewed probation, diversion or community service for drug offenders. There was a war on drugs, and they intended to be front-line warriors in the battle. I didn't know what to expect, and my legal aid lawyer didn't tell me. I pleaded guilty and was sentenced to nine months in prison for possession of heroin. Of course, a small-town beauty queen who was a drug addict was fair game for a media hungry for scandal, and everyone jumped on it: radio, newspaper and television. What did my family say? What did they think? I'll never know, because it was never discussed. Indeed, throughout my incarceration, my family never came to see me, save one visit from my mom.

Oakalla Prison was decrepit, cold and frightening. There had been a recent policy change that allowed women with long federal sentences to do their time there. I was surrounded by hardened criminals: drug smugglers, murderers, bank robbers, mostly addicted women, and a smattering of elderly Doukhobors, a sect of Russian immigrants who called themselves the Sons of Freedom and settled mainly in British Columbia and Saskatchewan. To show their disdain of the material world, these women stripped naked, burned their own homes, and torched public buildings, rail lines, and schools in protest over governmental education policies.

Music blared all day in the women's unit, and one song by Skylark, a Canadian pop group, was played over and over again. To this day it touches me like no other pop song:

# Wildflower

She's faced the hardest times you can imagine
And many times her eyes fought back the tears
And when her youthful world was about to fall in
Each time her slender shoulders
Bore the weight of all her fears
And a sorrow no one hears
Still rings in midnight silence
in her ears
Let her cry, for she's a lady
Let her dream, for she's a child

Let the rain fall down upon her
She's a free and gentle flower
growing wild
And if by chance that I should hold her
Let me hold her for a time
But if allowed just one possession
I would pick her from the garden to be mine
Be careful how you touch her for she'll awaken
And sleep's the only freedom that she knows
And when you walk into her eyes you won't believe
The way she's always paying for a debt she never owes
And a silent wind still blows that only she can hear
And so she goes
Let her cry, for she's a lady
Let her dream, for she's a child
Let the rain fall down upon her
She's a free and gentle flower
growing wild[3]

I was a well-behaved inmate, but the officers discovered that I possessed a bottle of "downers." Funny thing was that I never took a pill; I simply held on to them in case I needed to, like an insurance policy. The officers sent me to the "hole" for a week. Yes, solitary confinement: a steel door, no windows, a thin blanket and a bright light bulb that hurt my eyes. Eventually I was transferred to a work farm in Maple Ridge called Twin Maples. This was an open dorm correctional centre—no locks and no bars. But like the Eagles sang in "Hotel California," "You can check out anytime you like, but you can never leave."

Eventually, near the end of my sentence, I obtained a work release, which meant that three days a week a male guard drove me to a crummy coffee shop in Maple Ridge where all the next-door Safeway employees took their coffee breaks. It was humiliating, as it was well known that every new waitress was a prison inmate. Later this same guard picked me up from the café and drove me and an attractive blonde inmate to his

[3] "Wildflower" is written by David Richardson and Doug Edwards. Copyright Edsel Music 1972, renewed 2000. Used by permission. Administered by Nettwerk One Music (Canada) Ltd. www.wildflowersong.com.

home. I was the third wheel, waiting in his car while he and the blonde went into his house to have sex—shades of *Orange Is the New Black*.

When my sentence was finished, I was given money to travel to Nanaimo to live and to pay room and board to a family willing to take me in, an accommodation secured for me by prison officials. I knew I couldn't return to New Westminster or the suburbs of Vancouver, the scene of the crime. Soon afterward I began working as a cocktail waitress at a local nightclub. I also picked up a new—and abusive—boyfriend.

Determined to rise above these circumstances, I moved to Metro Vancouver to complete my three-year probation period. I worked as a dental assistant but quickly realized that the restaurant business was far more lucrative for a young, energetic girl—and much more fun! I worked at several fine-dining restaurants and learned how to serve VIP guests and how to open wine. I even learned how to cook from some of Vancouver's best chefs. In the early '80s I worked at Avanti on the Plaza at the Lougheed Mall in Coquitlam and was awarded "Waiter of the Year" by the British Columbia Restaurant Association.

In part, I attribute my ability to overcome many challenges to my energy and passion. Is it possible to be a visionary leader without passion? Resoundingly no! Passion is what drives a person to investigate opportunities, to boldly inspire others and to create contagious energy for a project or a business. You must love what you do. The apostle Paul wrote in Colossians 3:23, "Whatever you do, work heartily, as for the Lord and not for men." A large part of my early success was my overwhelming passion for what I was learning and doing. For me, passion coupled with hard work and commitment was a winning formula.

While I was working at Puccini's Restaurant in Vancouver, a workmate informed me that the charter airline Wardair was hiring stewardesses. I had never considered a career as a flight attendant, but I showed up, filled out the forms and was interviewed, and within days I was told to pack my bags for Toronto. I quit my job, stored my apartment furniture at my parents' place and left my little red Triumph Spitfire on the street in front of their home.

I was excited to start a new adventure but heartbroken to leave behind my new boyfriend, a City of Vancouver police officer. Doug and I exchanged many letters as I travelled the world. Life was grand until I returned to Vancouver about a year later. With sheer joy, I embraced Doug, twirling around him, excited to be home. But Doug wasn't smiling; he was very serious. He said our relationship was over. I was shocked. Why? I asked. He told me that his close friend, also a police officer, had given him a photo of me. It was a mug shot. I cried for days. I was shaken to my core.

I continued to fly with Wardair, and I met a young man from a wealthy family in Vancouver. We moved in together and two years later married. Two weeks before the wedding, I knocked on Doug's door and told him I was getting married. I begged him to stop me. He didn't.

The marriage lasted less than 12 months. But that wasn't all. Before the wedding, I was fired from Wardair. The application form I had filled out two years earlier asked whether I had a criminal record. Of course, I said no. If I had answered truthfully I would not have been hired. Now a young lawyer working for the flight attendants' union said there was no recourse for me. I was devastated. I had no money, no friends, no job, no education, no prospects and no husband. Nothing!

Thus was my ignominious launch into adulthood and an apt place to contemplate whether those who falter can pick themselves up and emerge as leaders. At the time, I didn't think so. I always believed that leadership was reserved for the intellectuals, the emotionally secure and the ones who grew up in a "good" family, awash with business and community connections, surrounded by people who could open doors as they were mentored and encouraged. But from these difficult years, and as I matured, I learned an important lesson in leadership.

## LEADERS LEARN FROM FAILURES

Leaders learn more from their failures than from their successes. The adage that "failure is not an option" couldn't be further from the truth. Failure teaches you about survival, renewal and reinvention of yourself or the organization you are leading. Fear of failure is also a huge stumbling block on the road to success. In Nelson Mandela's words: "Do not judge me by my successes, judge me by how many times I fell down and got back up again."[4] The most revered men of God, including Abraham, Moses, Elijah, David and Peter, stumbled and fell, but they recovered to bring great honour to themselves and God. I'm convinced that the bad decisions I made in my late teens and early twenties gave me the motivation, drive

---

[4] Nelson Mandela, quoted in Ann Kannings, *Nelson Mandela: His Words* (Raleigh: Lulu Press, 2014).

and, frankly, the desperation to pick myself up and show the world that I was not that person.

After my divorce was finalized I moved to Vancouver and went back into the restaurant business. It was there that I met a waitress who had a university degree. It now seems hard to believe, but I had never met a person with a university education—and she didn't seem that much smarter than me!

I did two things that week. I registered for classes at Burnaby's Simon Fraser University, and I started attending Broadway Pentecostal Church in East Vancouver. I was 30 years old.

I chose a criminology major, an area that fascinated me, probably because of my earlier passion for *True Detective* magazines and my experience with the criminal justice and correctional system. In two years, after taking six semesters back to back, with full course loads, I had a bachelor of arts in criminology and the highest marks in my graduating class. To my delight, Doug and I reunited, and he was back in my life.

As my final year rolled around, many of my schoolmates, most about ten years younger than me, were talking about law school and LSAT scores. My earlier thoughts of teaching school were swept aside when I realized that the 1980s' economy had been brutal on the teaching profession: lots of teachers and no jobs. So I wrote my LSAT and applied to the local University of British Columbia Law School.

I began law school in 1985. It was challenging and very tough! I worked three jobs, obtained more student loans and began singing and writing again. I was senior editor of the *Canadian Journal of Family Law*, did editorial work for the *Canadian Bar Review* and worked at Vancouver's Joe Fortes Restaurant three nights a week.

Along the way, I learned that ability and talent were only small parts of building professional success. What was really required was long, hard work, commitment and passion. You may be incredibly gifted, but without long hours and hard work your superior skills will be for naught. A seven-foot-tall basketball player who couch surfs all day and gorges on ice cream will probably never play on an NBA team, while his much shorter brother who has less physical prowess but works his butt off and loves the game may make the all-star game. Hard work and commitment outscore talent every time.

The year 1988 was big: I graduated from law school, married Doug and learned another big lesson: You are never too old to reimagine your life. At 35 I was embarking on the biggest challenge I ever faced: becoming a lawyer. While my law school colleagues were approaching their mid-twenties, I was getting close to middle-aged, and believe me, 27 years ago, 35 was considered old.

I took a tip from Mark Twain: "Age is an issue of mind over matter. If you don't mind, it doesn't matter," and I approached my new career with excitement and gusto. My age was never an issue. In fact, I believe my life experiences and late entry into academia contributed to my career success. As I encounter today's millennials who think that it's too late to start something new, I assure them that it is never too late. After all, Julia Child was 49 when she published *Mastering the Art of French Cooking*, and British vocalist Susan Boyle rocked the world at age 48, launching a singing career. Leaders understand that age is never a stumbling block. You are not too young or too old to create a vision for yourself, follow through and dream big.

Of course, I had challenges, plenty of them. It wasn't until I graduated that I began to think about how my past would affect my future. I was never very close to my law professors, but I approached one and briefly explained my situation. With unbridled disdain, he asked me how I could have possibly thought I was suitable for the practice of law. It was actually a very good question, because he was right; I had never thought about it. I thought that the federal pardon I received sealed the door shut on that episode of my life.

Many years later this same professor became a judge in Vancouver. He travelled to a law conference in New Zealand where he met my aunt, my mom's sister, who was a lawyer in Christchurch. She immediately asked if he knew her niece Georgialee Lang. He answered affirmatively and, ironically, regaled my aunt with my reputation and accomplishments in the bar. So much for my unsuitability!

After working as a judicial law clerk for a year I started my articles with BigLaw, and again those darn forms needed to be filled out! I had learned my lesson with Wardair and used pages of foolscap to recount my early history, giving the completed documents to a senior partner. I worried for more than a week, expecting the partner to dismiss me before the Law Society could do so. He didn't say a word to me, and interestingly, I later represented him during his divorce.

BigLaw was an amazing place to work. Because I had clerked, my articles lasted only four months, and I was called to the bar in November 1989. They offered me a position as an associate lawyer in commercial litigation. I was thrilled, but I wanted to practice family law. I convinced them that I could initiate and develop a new family law practice, but until that occurred I would work in estate litigation with their wills and estates department. They gently tried to dissuade me, but I wasn't having any of it. So it began, with an email to each of the firm's 110 lawyers: "I'm Georgialee Lang. I'm doing family law. Please refer your clients to me." And they did!

Within three years, BigLaw moved me into the corner office of a departed partner. I had a black marble desk and elegantly panelled hardwood walls, but best of all I had a spectacular view of Stanley Park, Coal Harbour and the snow-topped mountains of North and West Vancouver. My practice grew quickly, and now I had a full-time paralegal, a secretary, and a full-time junior lawyer working with me.

෪

My success eventually presented me with a big decision: stay at BigLaw or start my own business. At such crossroads, you realize that leaders must be able to make decisions, follow through and stand by their decisions. Leaders must be confident enough to take risks in order to see growth, and they must admit when they are wrong. Leaders never "pass the buck"; they are responsible for their team and graciously share the success of their leadership with others. A strong leader has the confidence to surround herself with smart people who have skills she doesn't have and to share the limelight. "Do not throw away your confidence, which has a great reward" (Hebrews 10:35). And so I decided to leave BigLaw (with as much confidence as I could muster) and search out the best team possible.

In October 1994 I opened my boutique firm in Vancouver across from the Supreme Court, with one paralegal and one secretary. Three months later I added my first associate. Gratefully, I took almost 100 clients with me, as upon my departure BigLaw stopped doing family law and referred their clients to me.

One opportunity led to another. A local talk show host at BC's biggest radio station invited me to come on his show to talk about family law. The phone lines lit up, mainly because it seemed that no family escaped this dreaded dilemma of family problems. Soon other media outlets, including television, print media, and more radio stations, were clamouring for me to talk about the popular topics: child custody, Christmas access, child support, spousal support, parental alienation, shared parenting, child abduction and, later, same-sex marriage. I began guest-hosting radio shows with political themes, and later I was offered my own morning talk show.

My law practice quickly grew to include five lawyers, multiple staff and paralegals, an IT guy and a bookkeeper-accountant. I began to realize that true leadership entailed mentoring, encouraging and supporting the professional growth and development of my employees.

## LEADERS MUST MENTOR

Mentoring is a two-way street. It provides extraordinary opportunities to facilitate an employee's personal and professional growth by sharing knowledge learned through years of experience. However, leaders also benefit from mentoring as they enhance their skills, facilitate their own growth, learn to manage people and strengthen their coaching and leadership skills. A savvy businesswoman mentors to develop and retain talent to grow her business and provide opportunities for others to succeed. You can create a legacy by sharing your values, principles and mission with younger employees. I learned to "walk the ship," pausing to say a personal hello to each staff member every morning, a simple act that underscored their value to me.

As my reputation grew in the legal community I began fielding calls from my contemporaries and junior lawyers who needed to be pointed in the right direction. As a leader, I have an obligation to share my expertise and knowledge with my colleagues—even, dare I say it, with my competitors! A true leader does not hoard information but willingly spreads it around. With the pastors and junior lawyers who asked for help, a win-win situation was created. They were in a position to move forward in their roles, and I was able to establish my credibility and expertise with a larger audience.

Now I'm not suggesting that you give away trade secrets or confidential strategies or work for free (although at times you will want to); rather I'm saying that a successful leader gives back and, in turn, reaps enormous personal and professional benefits.

Further, a leader does not hide away in her office but must engage in professional and charitable associations, for two simple reasons. The first is that as a privileged member of the community, a lawyer (or any other professional or businesswoman) has been blessed with the opportunity to obtain a specialized education, and to whom much is given, of her much is expected (see Luke 12:48). The second is that true leaders are not just leaders in their workplace but also leaders in their communities, churches, sports fields and all the other places a leader frequents. For working moms this can be quite a challenge, and it might mean that their volunteer work revolves around their children's activities. What would soccer fields, baseball diamonds, and hockey rinks do without the help of moms who can coach, supervise, organize and audit, just a few of the roles a leader plays in the community?!

As community and professional involvement increase, opportunities are bound to show up, and for me that occurred in 2000 when I was invited to be an adjunct professor at the University of British Columbia Law School, teaching family law. I served at the law school for six years, teaching hundreds of students what I had learned over more than ten years of practicing law. I likely would have continued, but I received bombshell news. I had hepatitis C and had probably been infected for more than 30 years. It wasn't a big shock; how could it be? I had shared dirty needles for two years on the streets of Vancouver. I was just grateful that the HIV virus didn't arrive in Vancouver until the early '80s.

My doctors told me there was no cure; it was considered a fatal disease. I would eventually be struck down by either cirrhosis of the liver or liver cancer, both most unpleasant. I had never had any symptoms, but that's usually the case. I was told that medical scientists worldwide were looking for a treatment that would stave off the inevitable.

In late 2003, I received a call from my gastroenterologist. American researchers had discovered that a cocktail of chemotherapy drugs gave patients a fifty-fifty chance of a complete cure. There was more. A pilot project at St. Paul's Hospital in Vancouver was underway where the drugs were being tested on 30 individuals. The only problem was that there were no openings for additional patients. As the drugs had not been approved in Canada, I could purchase them for $37,000 for the eleven-month treatment. Before we had time to think about my options, St. Paul's Hospital called. A patient had dropped out...would I like to fill the space? Would I!

Thus began the hardest time of all. As a self-employed lawyer I never even considered taking time off. I trudged to the office and the courthouse just as before, but within five months of commencing treatment I lost 20 pounds. I couldn't eat. Nothing appealed to me, and with gaping mouth sores it was just not worth the discomfort. A month or so later, all my hair had fallen out.

It was an awful time. I had a two-week trial in New Westminster and couldn't even make it up the grand staircase outside the heritage courthouse. I completed the trial but only with the help of my legal assistant, who met me every day, helped me up the stairs and stayed close by me. God bless her! I suffered from minor "brain fog," as is common with chemotherapy, but I knew the law and I loved to litigate, and that saved me. When I was working I didn't feel sick, but I collapsed as soon as I returned home. It got so bad that Doug told me that several mornings he was tempted to call an ambulance to take me to the hospital. Towards the end of the treatment, my white cell count was so poor that I was given more drugs, with the advice that if I didn't improve, they would take me off chemotherapy completely. I would never let that happen. I needed this fifty-fifty chance.

The biggest mistake I made during this trying time was pretending that everything was fine. I didn't let my professional colleagues know I was ill, but it was becoming very obvious. The cure was worse than the disease! My pastor and some church friends knew, as did my legal assistant. I didn't tell any other friends or anybody in my family. My parents were aging, but I didn't visit them for 11 months. I couldn't let them see me in the condition I was in.

## LEADERS ARE AUTHENTIC

I believed that if my friends, family and professional colleagues knew I was sick and on chemo, they would look at me differently. I would lose my edge—a fate I needed to avoid at all costs. But I was wrong. A hallmark of true leadership is authenticity and the ability to unabashedly ask for help when it's needed. When I was forced to admit I was suffering, I expected rejection, but I received support. My fear of judgment and condemnation was unwarranted. I learned a hard lesson: "No woman is an island."

Four months into treatment, my weekly blood tests indicated that the virus had disappeared. That was terrific, but relapses were more common than not. I needed to be free of the virus for a year after treatment ended to be declared "cured."

Apart from the physical side effects, the worst part was the emotional and psychological fallout. My family doctor had predicted major emotional issues, and besides the chemo, I was on depression meds, anti-anxiety prescriptions and other assorted drugs. I should say here that after entering prison I had never used any drugs, nothing! Now I was on all these "crazy" pills, and boy, did I need them.

I found a Christian therapist, and she became my saviour. It was my first time in therapy. What I learned about myself was mind-boggling! She diagnosed me with post-traumatic stress syndrome, arising from the events of the past that I had never dealt with. I also had a generalized anxiety disorder. Say what? I thought I was normal, that my hyper energy, my overwhelming drive and ambition, was who I was.

After 11 months of torture, the chemo was finally over. I was clear, no virus. I thought I'd be fully recovered within six months, but my doctor said it would take two to three years. I didn't believe her, but she was right. In the aftermath of chemotherapy I learned that my thyroid was trashed and my adrenal glands spent. I was diagnosed with adrenal fatigue, a situation that drained the last vestiges of energy my body possessed. With the help of a doctor who specialized in burnout, I began a regimen of homeopathic and naturopathic treatments, ignoring her advice that I take a year off work. I did spend two months recovering at our summer home in the Okanagan, only to return to find out that two of my associate lawyers had given their notice. Ah...the joys of running a business!

By now, my life had changed completely. I was a different person. Life-threatening events tend to shake people up, and my world was topsy-turvy. I had been aloof, with a posture of "perfection," but I knew I could never go back to the arm's-length life I had been leading.

I also experienced a feeling of compassion for others, something that frankly had been foreign to me. As a kick-ass trial lawyer, there wasn't a lot of room for sympathy or empathy, but my chemo journey taught me a lot about suffering and underscored for me the charmed life I was living despite my earlier setbacks.

☙

As I sat in church one Sunday morning, I asked God what He wanted me to do. His answer was almost immediate. Because I started my career at BigLaw and then developed a high-end family law practice, I had never worked with the disadvantaged, the poor, the mentally ill—the most vulnerable people in society, people who could never afford a lawyer, the ones turned away from legal aid, the most hopeless cases.

In March 2005 I started a pro bono law clinic at Broadway Church in Vancouver, where once a month a line formed at the door at 3 p.m. for the 6 p.m. start of the clinic. I provided legal advice to many hundreds of clients during the clinic's five-year run, many who made repeat visits as their legal issues wound through the court system. I stayed until the last client had been served, often as late as 11 p.m.

The joy I experienced over the five years my clinic ran was indescribable. These clients, who had nothing, were the most grateful, the most hopeful, the most resilient people I had encountered in my years of practicing law.

Over the years I authored many academic articles and edited several legal publications, but I felt a yearning to write for the "folks." In May 2010 I began my blog *Lawdiva*, where I cover a diverse range of legal and political topics, including stories about judges, lawyers, criminal law, family law, wrongful convictions, pop culture and legal ethics.

And the Lord's blessings continued to flow. If you're a research scientist, the highest honour is a Nobel Prize; if you're a skater, your aim is the Olympics; and if you're a trial lawyer, you can only hope that one day you'll appear as counsel in the Supreme Court of Canada. I was blessed with three opportunities to argue in front of the "Supremes," in 2008, 2009 and 2013.

After my second appearance I was invited to join the Supreme Court of Canada Advocacy Institute, where selected Canadian lawyers make themselves available to assist their colleagues who are scheduled to appear before the court, to give them coaching and encouragement before what can be a daunting, even frightening, prospect. Invitations like this become available as one's reputation grows.

## LEADERS EARN THEIR REPUTATIONS

A leader's reputation is something that must be earned, one day at a time. I found that as I began to fine-tune my leadership skills, my growth and maturity were directly connected to my goal to achieve excellence and in turn become an influencer in my profession.

In order for you to lead and influence, people have to want to follow you, and they will if you are a person they can trust to lead the way, a leader who demonstrates not just competence but the highest skill levels.

I'm not talking about technical or operational skills; you can hire people for that. I mean ability, continuously honed, to keep learning, to understand the issues and to evaluate talent. Proverbs 3:21 reads, "Do not lost sight of these—keep sound wisdom and discretion."

However, competence must be accompanied by excellence. Leaders do not accept second best. They strive to develop cutting-edge strategies, create productive work environments and ensure that their output is delivered to the marketplace with integrity and distinction. Romans 12:2 says, "Do not be conformed to this world, but be transformed by the renewal of your mind, that by testing you may discern what is the will of God, what is good and acceptable and perfect."

To my good fortune, the reputation I was developing led to one of my most interesting and challenging Supreme Court of Canada cases: *Attorney-General v. Bedford.* This was an Ontario case brought by a group of sex workers, represented by Professor Alan Young from Osgoode Hall Law School. They sought to convince our highest court that prostitution should be legalized across Canada. In 2012, I was retained by the Evangelical Fellowship of Canada to obtain "intervenor" status and, if successful, to argue against the legalization of prostitution. Intervenors are very common in the Supreme Court of Canada and other appellate courts, where interested organizations with expertise in issues relevant to an appeal are granted permission to submit written argument and, in some circumstances, deliver oral argument to the court.

The Evangelical Fellowship had long championed the fight against human trafficking, a particularly heinous adjunct to the world's oldest profession. I argued against permitting prostitution to flourish in Canada uninhibited by laws. My research revealed unequivocal evidence that in countries where prostitution was legal, human trafficking had exploded, with all of the dire consequences that accompany the degradation and subversion of girls and women who become exploited victims.

Professor Alan Young filed a motion asking the court to strike out a large portion of my written argument. But on the morning of June 13, 2013, as protesters waved banners in support of legal prostitution and Canada's national media outlets converged in front of the stately court house in Ottawa, Chief Justice Beverley McLachlin announced to a courtroom crowded with black-robed lawyers that his motion was dismissed.

With great relief I later stood before the court and delivered my entire argument. Of course, we all know how it turned out. The Supreme Court of Canada struck down Canada's prostitution laws, deeming them unconstitutional, saying that the criminalization of street solicitation, brothels and people living off the avails of prostitution created unsafe situations for vulnerable women.

Undaunted, I continued my advocacy work, publishing pieces on Canada.com and in the *Huffington Post* decrying our nation's insensitivity to the girls, women and young boys who are used and then tossed aside by sexual predators. As the government began to formulate new prostitution laws, I was invited to make oral submissions to the House of Commons Justice and Human Rights Committee. Among the speakers were victims of prostitution who had escaped the indignity and degradation of the sex trade, battle-scarred women who spoke out against the legalization of prostitution and urged the government to adopt a new criminal model. Based on Swedish law, advocates against legal prostitution urged politicians to enact laws where girls, women and young boys would no longer be arrested, but pimps would be prosecuted for living off the earnings of prostitutes, and customers who purchased sex would be arrested.

I too favoured an approach that recognized sex workers as exploited victims and criminalized those who took advantage of their vulnerabilities. Victims of prostitution include girls and women who are addicted to drugs, mentally ill, emotionally damaged, sufferers of child sexual abuse, Asian and Eastern European women who are trafficked and end up as so-called escorts, and marginalized aboriginal women, like some of those who were brutally murdered by British Columbia's serial killer Robert (Willy) Pickton. During the committee hearing, a New Democrat Party member of Parliament was quick to advise me, even taunt, that no other Canadian lawyer had espoused the position I was advancing. I told her that my position might not be popular among lawyers, but it was the right one!

Later I was invited to speak before the Senate Standing Committee on Legal and Constitutional Affairs, and lo and behold, the only two speakers on the agenda on the final day of hearings were Professor Alan Young and I. Needless to say, we had not bridged the gap between our polarized positions. It was déjà vu as he eloquently advanced the arguments he had made in the Supreme Court of Canada, and I, likewise.

⌘

As I began to open my heart to others I recognized that the next phase of my journey would not accommodate the legal rat race that had consumed my energy and focus for so many years. I wanted to offer legal services for free. I wanted to make a gift of my blessings to others. I was fortunate to be able to sell my law practice to a fine lawyer, a family man, with integrity and passion for men and women who were often at the lowest points in their life.

But then another constitutional issue came along that would not permit me to sit on the sidelines. Trinity Western University in British Columbia spent hundreds of hours jumping through the required governmental "hoops" to initiate a private Christian law school on their beautiful Langley campus, a first in Canada. They obtained the required permission from Canada's Federation of Law Societies and British Columbia's Ministry of Advanced Education. However, dissenting voices alleged that Trinity's proposed law school did not promote "equality and justice." Critics denounced Trinity's "community covenant" that called for the abstention from sexual intimacy that violates the sacredness of marriage between a man and a woman. This was characterized as an anti-gay stance, with most naysayers ignoring that the prohibition of sex outside of marriage also applied to unmarried heterosexual couples.

A flurry of lawsuits was launched, and disappointingly, BC's Ministry of Advanced Education withdrew their approval. Well-known Toronto criminal lawyer Clayton Ruby, who led the legal challenge against Trinity, said, "Almost the entire legal profession in Canada and in BC has repudiated the fanciful assertion that fundamentalist Christianity requires and justifies such behaviour."[5] Of course, the "behaviour" Mr. Ruby referred

---

[5] Clayton Ruby, quoted in Andrea Woo, "B.C. Revokes Consent for Controversial Law School," *The Globe and Mail*, December 11, 2014. Available at http://www.theglobeandmail.com/news/british-columbia/bc-revokes-consent-for-law-school-at-trinity-western-university/article22058567/.

to was the right of a private Christian educational institution to initiate a law school that upheld a biblical view of marriage.

Eventually the matter came before the elected benchers (governors) of the Law Society of British Columbia. The issue became "Would the Law Society permit graduates of Trinity University's proposed law school to article in BC?" In Canada law students cannot become lawyers until they have "articled" with a law firm or government agency.

Arguments for and against were vigorously argued, and it concluded with a 21 to 6 vote in favour of Trinity's law school. But the victory was short-lived and the matter far from over.

A small group of gay and lesbian lawyers, unhappy with the benchers' decision, called upon the Law Society to organize a meeting to permit a vote of its lawyer members. The inflammatory rhetoric of Trinity opponents was shocking coming from lawyers who swore an allegiance to the rule of law, as they referenced the Holocaust and suggested that Trinity law school graduates would share the qualities of members of the Nazi party and depraved criminals.

The few lawyers in favour of Trinity's law school relied on the law, reminding their colleagues that the British Columbia Human Rights Code specifically exempts religious groups, who are free to practice their faith. They confirmed that Canada's Charter of Rights and Freedoms did not apply to private educational institutions, as its purview of protection is against unfair governmental actions. They relied on the Supreme Court of Canada's earlier decision in *Trinity Western University v. BC College of Teachers* where the teacher's college tried to block Trinity-educated teachers from becoming members and teachers in BC and failed.

Ultimately, an overwhelming majority of lawyers in attendance voted against Trinity's law school, which brought the matter to a learned judge of the British Columbia Supreme Court, who heard arguments in August 2015. In December 2015 B.C's Chief Justice Hinkson overturned the lawyers' "no" vote, a ruling that was upheld by British Columbia's Court of Appeal. Alas, the Law Society has appealed our Court of Appeal's ruling to the Supreme Court of Canada, so we have not yet heard the "fat lady sing."

Not surprisingly, lawyers in other provinces also voted against Trinity, and each of these cases are now before the courts. The Nova Scotia Supreme Court thankfully held that allowing the Barristers Association's rejection of Trinity law students to stand would have a "chilling effect on the liberty of conscience and freedom of religion in Canada." The Ontario Court held that barring a Christian law school was a breach of religious rights, but it was a reasonable infringement, and it upheld the Law Society's decision to refuse to accept Trinity law school students as articling students. New Brunswick ruled in favour of Trinity. These mixed reviews of Trinity's law school make it even more certain there will be years of litigation until the Supreme Court of Canada resolves the issue. For now, the law school is on hold. Delay, of course, favours those opposing the law school.

People on both sides of this case demonstrate that leaders have influence. I believe that leaders should use their influence to advance causes that are important to them. One of the side effects of being a successful leader is that as respect grows, so does the ability to persuade, convince and even cajole others of the righteousness of a particular position, organization or social issue. It often takes courage to take a stand on a controversial issue, but being "true to yourself" has its own rewards. I believe the best leaders boldly step out when others are afraid to speak. Leaders should defend and advocate for the vulnerable, the underprivileged, for those who have become disposable because of age, addiction, mental illness or other causes. Leaders must love justice and loathe corruption and dishonesty.

&#8531;

Now I am able to pick and choose my cases. My law practice has also become international in scope, including clients whose partners have absconded with their children, invoking the Hague Convention on Child Abduction to obtain their return. I spend most of my time on cases from China, Taiwan, Portugal, the United Kingdom, Dubai and other faraway locations where there is a Canadian connection.

As a family law lawyer for 27 years, I saw the admirable efforts of all participants in the justice system to bring their "A" game to the table; however, I could not help but notice how Canadian families were being destroyed by the process. In a 2011 *Huffington Post* article I wrote,

> Our adversarial court system pits husband against wife in a dangerous game that all too often spirals out of control, taking whole families down and destroying children's lives in the process.

Custody cases are among the worst. Separating parents, usually fathers, are caught in a black vortex, fighting for the ability to remain an active part of their children's lives, sparring with mothers who too frequently use their hurt and anger to alienate their partners from their children.[6]

I continue writing and speaking on the benefits of shared parenting. In 2014 Canada.com and *The Lawyers Weekly* published my piece on the case for shared parenting where I wrote,

Despite the best efforts of dinosaur lawyers and jaded feminists to disparage a better model for parenting, shared parenting, also known as joint physical custody, is a child-centred response to the institutionalized model of parenting that has plagued families far too long. Based on twentieth century cultural traditions of stay-at-home moms and working dads, the maternal preference was shored up by untested psychological theories about mothers and children that unwittingly led to a template of a "visiting" parent, usually relegated to every second weekend for a total of four nights per month...Good parents were lumped in with dysfunctional parents because judges relied on precedent, a straight-jacket that we now know has hurt generations of children and needlessly disempowered parents.[7]

As a result of my shared parenting advocacy I was invited to join Leading Women for Shared Parenting, an American organization that recruits leaders from around the world who believe that the marginalization of fathers is decimating families and destroying children. I am happy to stand with my colleagues who are experts in their fields, including journalists, social workers, psychiatrists, attorneys, senators, television hosts and anchors, professors, doctors, elected members of legislatures, authors and domestic violence professionals.

---

[6] Georgialee Lang, "Who Will Fix Canada's Family Law System?" *The Huffington Post Canada*, June 29, 2011. Available at http://www.huffingtonpost.ca/georgialee-lang/family-law_b_884651.html.

[7] Georgialee Lang, "The Case for Shared Parenting," Canada.com, February 23, 2014. Available at http://o.canada.com/life/the-case-for-shared-parenting. Also, Georgialee Lang, "The Case for a 50-50 Shared Parenting Model," *The Lawyer's Weekly*, April 11, 2014, 11.

All of these challenges, opportunities and life moments take me back to where I started: the miracle of God's grace to change lives, open doors, provide physical and spiritual healing, bring the peace that passes understanding and, finally, turn those who feel lost into leaders. The Old Testament refers to the Hebrew word for grace, *chesed*, denoting deliverance from enemies, affliction or adversity. It also encompasses guidance, forgiveness and preservation. Grace is simply compassion and benevolence to the undeserving, to you and to me, freely given.

*Grace, mercy, and peace will be with us, from God the Father and from Jesus Christ the Father's Son, in truth and love.* (2 John 1:3)

---

 Georgialee Lang has been a trial and appellate lawyer for 28 years. A graduate of the University of British Columbia's law school, Georgialee is a Canadian leader in the family law bar and was recognized in 2013 with a prestigious Lexpert Zenith award, making her one of 60 Canadian women lawyers honoured for leadership in the profession. Georgialee has been recognized in *The Best Lawyers in Canada* in family law for the past 12 years.

Georgialee was an adjunct professor at the University of British Columbia Faculty of Law for six years and assumed leadership positions in the Canadian Bar Association, Legal Services Society, Lawyers Benevolent Fund, Continuing Legal Education, Alpha in the Workplace and the board of governors for Regent College. She is a prolific writer and media commentator who pens the award-winning blog *Lawdiva*. Three appearances as counsel in the Supreme Court of Canada have been the highlight of Georgialee's legal career. Married to Doug Lang, she loves to sing.

# *Singing*

## of Life and Love

by Carolyn Arends

Quirky country songwriter Lyle Lovett once claimed that he became a recording artist because his personality required amplification. That's my story, too.

I was the shy teenager who whispered one-liners to my outgoing best friend at parties so she could repeat my jokes aloud and get the laugh. No one at those gatherings ever would have predicted that quiet, awkward Carolyn would end up with a career lived out on concert stages.

It started, I think, the day my dad brought home a bright orange guitar. I was ten. Together we learned the chords to "Hang Down Your Head Tom Dooley." And I was hooked. I'd already been taking piano lessons for a few years, and I'd already had a piece or two of prepubescent poetry printed in a school publication. But there was something about the guitar that linked my verse-writing head with my music-loving heart. Soon I'd written my first song, a paean to my mom for Mother's Day. It was corny, but it went over big on the home front.

When a painfully shy girl finds a way to speak, it's empowering and addictive. My second song, written for an ecology project at school, was entitled "Just a Little Acorn." Before long, the pastor at my small Baptist church was asking me on a semi-regular basis to write songs to go with his sermon topics. In their loving enthusiasm, my parents and church community were affirming and nurturing me into a lifelong vocation.

Still, back then I would never have said out loud—even to myself—that I wanted a career in music. Sure, I sang into my hairbrush and fantasized about Amy Grant showing up at my junior high school to "discover" me. But I was certain that a music career was the sort of thing that happened to extraordinary people, not shy, awkward kids like me.

I wouldn't even let myself major in music at university, choosing instead to focus on studies in psychology and English at Trinity Western University (although I did pick up some music credits here and there). Still, for a non-music major, I spent a lot of time in the piano rooms on campus. In my second year, a gregarious (and rather adorable) junior named Mark Arends asked if I would play a saxophone solo during a performance by his vocal group. The performance itself was a disaster—the group was used to singing a cappella and started the song in a non-key that no traditional instrument could accommodate. But a romance had begun. It was Mark who sat me down the summer before my senior year and said, "It's kind of obvious to everyone except you that you are meant to pursue music."

Two other critical things happened that summer. First, Mark asked me to marry him, and I had the good sense to say yes. Second, I went to a Christian artist seminar in Colorado and worked up the nerve to play some rough church-basement demos of my music for a publishing panel. The publishers were notoriously hard on fledgling songwriters, and they shredded my songs just like they did all the others. But afterwards, Andrea Whitaker—a panellist who worked for Benson Publishing in Nashville— handed me her card and told me she heard some potential. Within a year I was a college graduate, new wife and staff songwriter for Benson Music.

## YOUR WORK IS HOLY

The term "staff songwriter" is misleading. Despite the fact that I had a "publishing deal," no real money changed hands. But Benson was interested in having me write songs for other artists, so they flew me to Nashville quarterly and had me collaborate with more established songwriters.

One of those veteran tunesmiths was Niles Borop. Full of dreams and ambition, I asked Niles for his best advice. He didn't hesitate before responding with words that have shaped my vocation ever since. "Never waste a listener's time," he told me. "To reach out through radio waves and command three-and-a-half minutes of someone's attention is a holy thing. Your song can move them—it can make them laugh, cry, consider the things of God or see the world in a new light. Take it seriously."

A few years after that conversation, people would ask me what it was like to hear one of my songs on the radio for the first time. It was definitely exciting to hear my tunes floating out on the airwaves. But even more amazing was the first time an audience sang along spontaneously to one of my songs in concert. I realized with shock that they had committed some of my words to their hearts. A little piece of my journey had become a little part of theirs. To this day, it *still* blows me away when that happens.

Thanks to Niles, one of the first important leadership lessons I learned is that anything worth doing is worth doing to your utmost ability, especially if it affects other people. Entrepreneur Seth Godin claims, "The biggest cause of excellence is the story we tell ourselves about our work."[8] Niles told me that my work was holy.

## DON'T IMPRESS THEM, BLESS THEM

It was holy work that I relished, and slowly I began to make professional progress, landing songs on projects here and there. At first, I had no ambition to record music myself—I had terrible stage fright, and so writing songs for other artists seemed the perfect solution. But I soon learned that the strongest songs were the most personal, and the personal songs were harder to give away. Record executives were starting to inquire about me as an artist. I found myself at a crossroads. Did I want to sing my songs myself? Or was I just too shy for the life of a performer?

Exactly two years after I attended the music seminar in Colorado, I found myself back at the conference again. But this time, as a signed songwriter, I was sitting on the panels doing the critiquing. One afternoon I had a gap in my schedule, so I slipped into the back of a room where a stagecraft seminar was being taught by a performance consultant named Tom Jackson.

Tom was addressing the issue of stage fright. He claimed that performers often don't understand what audience members need from a

---

[8] Seth Godin, "Plenty More," *Seth's Blog*, June 17, 2015. Available at http://sethgodin.typepad.com/seths_blog/2015/06/plenty-more.html.

concert. "Singers think it's about the lights or their wardrobe or even their vocal range," he said. "But it's not really. Those things are all important ingredients in a performance, of course. But why the audience is really there is to be loved. They are looking for connection."

Tom's words instantly struck me as true. I thought about the concerts that had really moved me and realized they had been all about connection—those moments when it felt like the artist was singing to *me* about *my life.*

"If you find yourself on a stage," Tom was explaining, "your primary job is to love your audience." I was nodding. This made sense. (In my mind I was paraphrasing the apostle Paul, "If I sing with the tongues of angels and play with a killer band and have the best lighting and production, but have not love, I am nothing.")

Tom's next statement stopped me in my tracks: "The enemy of love is self-consciousness."

I thought about the ways self-consciousness had robbed me of connection, not only on stage but also in every facet of my life. My self-consciousness at the checkout line at the grocery store had kept me looking down instead of meeting the clerk's eye. It had kept me mumbling at parties instead of really getting to know any of the people there. My shyness was keeping me from loving people.

A few weeks after I heard Tom speak, I found myself trembling in the wings in a little music room called The Railway Club in Vancouver. I had agreed to perform at a songwriter's showcase, and the familiar symptoms of stage fright were making me feel miserable. But I took a deep breath and prayed, "God, tonight I don't want to be self-conscious. I want to love that audience out there, whoever they are. Please help."

Most progress in life is made incrementally, one small step leading to another in the sacred work of becoming. But that night was a rare quantum leap, a flip of a switch. I walked out on stage and found myself intensely curious about the people in the crowd. What kind of days had they had? What brought them to this dark little room on a Thursday night? I forgot about myself almost entirely, and, for the first time ever, I had a ball on stage. And, honestly, I've been having a ball on stage ever since.

Tom Jackson defines "loving your audience" as "the attitude of wanting to give everything you can for the benefit of each person in the room." In truth, "loving your audience" (or your constituents, students, congregation, staff, clients or customers) is the primary calling beneath all of our other tasks and duties. Any leader who recognizes that she has been placed where she is to bless people—rather than impress them—is wonderfully liberated. Self-consciousness is banished in such a paradigm.

## NEVER A ZERO-SUM GAME

Almost four years after embarking on that first publishing deal with Benson, I signed a recording contract with Reunion Records. A few record labels had expressed interest by that point, and I went with Reunion because they were the record label for an artist named Rich Mullins. Rich was known for anthems like "Awesome God" and "Step by Step." But I loved even more the quirkiness and vulnerability he showed on songs like "The Maker of Noses" and "Hold Me Jesus." You can imagine how quickly I said yes when I was asked if I wanted to launch the release of my first album by joining a 63-city tour, opening for Rich and soulful rocker Ashley Cleveland!

Since that initial tour with Rich, I've observed that most concert tours observe a natural hierarchy. The brightest lights and the crispest sound are reserved for the headliner, while opening acts need to soldier on through less than ideal conditions. But Rich took a different approach. Every night he started the evening by walking out on stage (often with his hair still wet from a pre-show jog and shower) and asking the audience to pay attention to his friend Carolyn. Not only did it make my job infinitely easier; it made the entire event more cohesive and rewarding for the audience.

Rich taught me about generous leadership. He showed me that creative endeavours do not have to be a zero-sum game. When one leader shines a light on another, it doesn't plunge her into darkness—it helps both her and the other shine a little brighter. I found myself thinking about Rich's open-handed style again last year, almost two decades later, when another generous artist (Canadian Steve Bell) and I inadvertently launched crowd-funding campaigns for new projects at the same time. Instead of seeing each other as the competition, we each enthusiastically promoted the other's campaign—and wound up each raising far more than I believe we would have had we not had each other's support.

## THE HIDDEN POTENTIAL OF YOUR WEAKNESSES

Back in 1995, touring with Rich also taught me something about the intimate relationship that exists in each of us between our personal strengths and weaknesses. Once, over a pre-concert plate of lasagna, Rich and I got talking about our mutual ineptitude at sports. He told me how isolated he had felt growing up as a weak basketball player in hoops-crazed Indiana. He had known from an early age that he wasn't going to be a contender, so he pulled himself out of the game, bitterly disappointing his father (or so it seemed to him at the time) and leaving Rich with a sense of being a little on the outside of things. That alienation, he claimed, stayed with him throughout his high school years.

But he'd poured all that angst into music. On a milestone birthday, Rich, like all the other kids in his family, received a cow. But where most of his siblings sold their cow in order to buy a car, Rich bought a piano.

I watched Rich perform 63 times on that tour, and not once was I left unmoved. What struck me most was his ability to connect almost instantly with the disenfranchised, the alienated and the marginalized— with anybody who had ever felt left out, which is to say with everybody. For who among us has never felt apart or alone? I am thankful that Rich was forced a little to the outside of things as a young man, because I suspect that his wonderfully skewed view of life (not to mention his keen awareness that we are strangers and aliens in this world) would not have developed any other way. Standing just left of centre, he saw piercingly into the middle of human experience and began to describe it in wise and funny and poetic and prophetic ways. All those hours he could have poured into shooting hoops he spent pounding on his piano, enfleshing in melodies and lyrics the things we have all felt but struggled to express.

It is a well-known leadership principle that we need to be aware of not only our strengths but also our weaknesses so that we can pinpoint our growth's edges and proactively manage our vulnerabilities. This is true, as far as it goes. But Rich taught me that we also need to see our weaknesses as gifts in and of themselves—as part of the complex swirl of spirit and experience and design that makes us who we are. Rich helped me see that while I needed to keep working on my shyness and self-consciousness (don't even get me started regarding my sports skills), I could also be thankful for my tendency towards introversion. That facet of my personality has fostered in me a rich interior life, a contemplative outlook and a love of literary language. It has made me, among other things, a songwriter. And it has made me...me.

"When I am weak, then I am strong," the apostle Paul was fond of saying (2 Corinthians 12:10). Life has taught me that lesson well—it takes painful confrontations with my own inadequacy and brokenness and aloneness to make me realize how much I need the help and wholeness and belongingness that only a relationship with God and other people can bring. But I am beginning to think that there is even more to this paradox of strength in weakness.

I love the fact that Jesus chose the salty apostle Peter—a guy whose big mouth got him into all kinds of trouble his whole life—as the cornerstone of the Church, confident that the mysterious machinations of grace would transform Peter's tendency to blurt things out into a great gift for proclaiming the truth.

In God's upside-down kingdom, our deepest inadequacies are not only accepted; they become our assets. We expect a God of power to obliterate our weaknesses. Instead we are more likely to encounter a God of love who finds impossibly creative ways to convert those liabilities into our best features. Only the Author of love could come up with a plot twist like this in the story of redemption—we actually become better not in spite of but *because* of our infirmities.

Was it Beethoven's physical deafness that enabled him to hear—uninterrupted—the glorious themes of his Ninth Symphony? Was it Milton's blindness that intensified his vivid interior vision of *Paradise Lost*? Could the poet Blake have given us the fearful symmetry of his "lamb" and "Tyger" with a less troubled mind? The great novelist Dostoyevsky claimed that his extraordinary insights were somehow connected to his epilepsy. And what about the apostle Paul—could he have taught all the believers after him that suffering leads to perseverance, character and, ultimately, hope if his pesky thorn had been removed?

I'm glad I learned early on in my journey the leadership lesson that, if we belong to God, wherever our greater brokenness lies, there also lies our greatest potential. These transformations are not easy—the truth is, they are often excruciatingly slow and painful. But they are real nonetheless, or at least they can be if we give every aspect of ourselves to our Maker to be recreated. Rich Mullins understood this, and playing music with him changed my life. When he died in a tragic car accident less than two years after our tour together, I knew that his own transformation was complete—and that I had been extraordinarily blessed to meet him along the way.

## GOOD LEADERSHIP IS MORE THAN THE SUM OF ITS PARTS

That tour (and the release of my first CD) took place in 1995. The next few years were a mostly happy blur of recording studios, tour buses and stages. Sometimes my bandmates and I found ourselves in larger-than-life situations, playing for audiences of 100,000 or more at festivals in the United States, England and Holland or opening for Steven Curtis Chapman and Audio Adrenaline in 90 packed basketball and hockey arenas across North America. Other times, we found ourselves in cozier settings, playing our music on smaller coffee house or church stages. In every instance, we tried to share our hearts just the way we would on a back porch or in a living room. Love was the goal.

Along the way we learned more and more about the power of connection—musician with musician, artist with audience, and all of us with the God in whom we "live and move and have our being" (Acts 17:28). Once, during a concert with my duo partner Spencer Capier at a beautiful little church in Eerie, Pennsylvania, I sang a song entitled "In Good Hands." Afterward, the church's custodian stopped by. "When you was singing that song about Jesus' hands," he said, "the sun was setting behind you, and it was making them stained glass pictures of Jesus glow. The sound of your buddy's violin was bouncing off these stone walls, and, well, you were saying more than you was even saying." He was reminding me that leadership always involves connection—to ourselves, to the created world, to each other and to God. When a leader discovers that her best work is greater than the sum of its parts, she is both humbled and inspired.

Throughout much of my music career, I've had a sense of awe about the gift of song and the way art in general can help us say more than we could say any other way. Sometimes I'll return to one of my own lyrics and have no idea how it was written. I often joke that I will never introduce one of my own tunes with the phrase "Here is a song God gave me," because I don't want the audience to hear the song and say, "Hmm, maybe because He didn't want it!" But I have to confess that, in the final analysis, any good work I have done transcends any abilities I may have. The best music (and, really, all of our best work) is sheer gift, and I am grateful.

$\infty$

My husband, Mark, was incredibly generous during those hectic years. He joined me on the road when he could, but there were long stretches apart. We missed each other terribly, but we both had a strong sense that God equips you for what He calls you to do. Mark kept busy, tackling his master's degree in educational counselling while continuing to work full-time as a teacher. Eventually he launched into his role as a high school counsellor in the public school system. I am constantly amazed by his ability to reach teenagers, tearing down walls and building up hope in the process. Whenever we go out, he gets recognized far more than I do, and I love hearing the familiar refrain of "Mr. A!"

Both Mark and I have always loved kids, and by 1997—the third year of my recording career and the eighth year of our marriage—we knew it was time to have some of our own. In February of 1998 Benjamin came along and redefined everything that matters for us, and his sister, Bethany, joined the party in 2001.

At first, I continued full-speed ahead with my music career, packing up the kids and taking them with me wherever I went. (To this day, if we haven't spent some time in a hotel in a while, they start to feel restless.) But soon, we could all see that something was going to get dropped in the balancing act. By the end of 2001, after four albums together, Reunion Records and I agreed that I could no longer be on the road as extensively as they required. We parted ways, and my own little label, 2B Records, was born.

It wasn't the end of the music. In the years since, I've recorded eight more projects (and counting), often in business collaboration with Steve Bell's Winnipeg-based Signpost Music. But taking things independent was an opportunity for me to limit travel to weekends and make the music accommodate family life a little more graciously.

That's not to say that we've always gotten the balance right. I often suffer from the classic working mom angst of feeling that both family and vocation are getting the short shrift. But it's worth struggling through the tension, because all of it matters. And one thing I've noticed in my journey is that often a hallmark of something that matters is that it doesn't come easily.

## THE IMPORTANCE OF TELLING YOUR STORY

Right around the time Mark and I were growing into our roles as parents, my career was branching out to include authorship. I'd always written prose here and there, and a letter that the record label had asked me to write to go with my third album seemed to connect with people almost as much as the album itself. Some editors at Harvest House Publishing asked if I would try my hand at writing a book, and a parallel vocation was launched.

Authoring a book was tricky. One of the key aspects of good songwriting is learning to purify and distill—a three-and-a-half minute song can really only be about one thing, so anything tangential has to be stripped away. Authorship is different. I realized that my book was going to take less than four minutes to read unless I switched gears and allowed myself to expand and explore—to go down side roads and back alleys. It turned out to be quite a journey.

The book was called *Living the Questions*, later republished as *Wrestling with Angels*. The genre was spiritual memoir, and it was basically a series of literary snapshots of moments from my life during which I had encountered the living God in some way. It operated on the hunch that our questions and longings have as much (maybe more) to tell us as do our answers and satisfactions. It was painfully vulnerable in places, and those places ended up being the spaces where the greatest connection occurred with readers.

The process of writing and releasing the book confirmed for me a suspicion I'd had for a long time as a songwriter—that one of our primary tasks while we are here on this planet is to tell our stories. In attending to our stories, we listen to our lives. We discover a billion points of connection with each other. And we begin to detect the hand of God moving in the minutiae of our days. As Neil Postman once said, "Without air, our cells die. Without a story, our selves die."[9]

## A JOURNEY OF DAILY DEPENDENCE

Telling my story in print led to requests for me to begin speaking at retreats and conferences. I received these requests with dread and all the old fear and self-consciousness that had originally paralyzed me on concert stages. But a friend named Rory Holland cornered me and told me I'd be speaking for a weeklong retreat at a gorgeous family camp on Keats Island, BC, called Barnabas.

Barnabas runs family camps all summer, and they set aside three hours each day for the adults to gather for teaching. I was to be the teacher. The

---

[9] Neil Postman, "Learning by Story," *Atlantic Monthly,* December 1989, 122.

catch (in addition to the fact that I didn't know how to be the teacher) was that this particular week of camp was a private rental by a group who had been attending for years as a kind of experiment. Half of the attendees were Christians, and half were not, and they were engaged in a good-natured but intense long-term debate over the real meaning of life. I had no idea what to say to them.

Every single night of that first camp, I stayed up until three or four in the morning, wrestling through the notes I had brought with me, crossing things out, scribbling in the margins. Every single night I eventually fell asleep, filled with despair, telling the Lord that I had no idea what I was going to talk about in the morning. And then, every single morning, I woke up with clarity about what we should talk about next, and the sessions would unfold in all sorts of surprising and wonderful ways. The whole process made me utterly dependent on the leading of the Spirit (and more than a little sleep deprived).

When Jesus' first-century disciples asked Him how they should pray, He told them to ask God not just "for bread" but for "*daily* bread" (Matthew 6:11). There's no doubt He was reminding them of the way their ancestors, recently delivered from Egyptian slavery, had been certain they were going to starve in the wilderness until God started providing them with a mystery food called "manna" (Exodus 16). God was generous with this manna but gave them clear instructions. They were never to hoard the food but rather to trust God to give them a fresh batch daily. The only exception was the eve of the Sabbath. On that day, they could store up enough manna to last them for the next 48 hours, and it would stay fresh. But any other day, if they tried to stash some of the food as a contingency plan, it would rot by the next morning. God's food-delivery system was ingenuous. It was also quite the object lesson.

My first time speaking at Camp Barnabas, struggling each night to discern where God was leading for the next morning, I was literally forced to rely on Him for my daily bread. The idea that sometimes God shines just enough light on your path to illuminate your next step became less of a greeting card cliché and more a matter of survival. That first speaking engagement led to many others—our family can hardly wait to return to Barnabas every year, and at this stage in my career, about 70 percent of my bookings involve speaking at camps, retreats, conferences and seminars. Happily, I have gradually become a more prepared, competent and confident presenter. But there is almost always a moment at every engagement when I am reminded that faithful leaders are only as effective as they are dependent on God.

I've had to learn that same lesson time and again on concert stages, too. A few years ago, I found myself feeling miserable in the midst of a tour. My own company was handling many of the details (a necessary complication of the choice to go independent), and every night I took the stage consumed with logistics. I've always loved the fact that performing forces me to be in the moment, but on this tour I was definitely somewhere else. I'd find myself disoriented in the middle of a song, unsure whether I'd already sung the second verse. Something was wrong.

I prayed. I asked God to restore to me the joy of singing about my salvation. I begged for the ability to be focused and present. And I worried. I suspected that the blessing of my vocation had run its course and that it was time for me to investigate Tupperware sales.

Three weeks into the tour, I lost my voice. This was, as you might imagine, a problem. I reminded God that it would be helpful to my singing ministry if I could sing. But my voice did not return. I called a vocal coach and got instructions. "Hourly, sit at a kettle and breathe in the steam. Then add salt to the water and snort it. Put drops of oil of oregano on your tongue. Apply peppermint oil to your upper lip." (Caution: Over-application of peppermint oil leads to a condition I remember now as "the moustache of fire.")

I spent 24 hours sequestered in my hotel room in an involuntary silent retreat. No interviews, no fretful logistical phone meetings. I steamed without end. By concert time, my skin had never been smoother or softer. But I still had no voice.

A funny thing happened when I took the stage. I felt calm and present. The whole quiet day I'd had nothing to do but steam, read and pray. A paraphrase of Psalm 23 ran through my head: You *make* me lie down by still waters—or steamy, salty ones. I walked up to the microphone and had a sudden conviction that my voice would be not only restored but also brilliantly transformed.

It wasn't. I still couldn't sing. Not a bit. I croaked, I cracked, I sort of whisper-rapped. It was awful. But the audience leaned in. They smiled. They prayed for me. Never certain what my swollen vocal cords would do next, I was in the moment, adapting, adjusting and—eventually—enjoying a new and improbably wonderful way of doing ministry. It was, to both my chagrin and my delight, one of my best concerts ever. And it was, for me, a rediscovery of the truth that the best leadership is reliant on a power far beyond the leader's own resources.

&#8471;

As my career has branched out from songwriter to recording artist, touring musician, independent record label owner, author, speaker and teacher, I've sometimes wondered if I've become too diffuse or scattered. I confessed that fear a few years ago to my friend, mentor and co-producer Roy Salmond. He smiled. "It's all communication," he said. "Sometimes you set it to music and you sometimes you don't. But you are always using language to try to invite people to think about things of ultimate importance."

Roy's one-word description of my vocation as "communication" has helped me settle into and embrace numerous additional opportunities. For many years I served as a film critic for *Christianity Today*, a popcorn-butter-soaked role that I relished. That writing relationship led eventually to a five-year standing column with the magazine, entitled "Wrestling with Angels," where I had free rein to explore matters of spiritual formation, church life and the intersection of faith and the arts. Meanwhile, my opportunities to teach at the college level have expanded to include courses in music, aesthetics, theology and worship. And lately I have relished launching into a new and incredibly exciting adventure as the director of education with Renovaré, an organization that exists to encourage and nurture intentional spiritual formation in all sorts of thoughtful ways.

## BE A RESERVOIR, NOT A CANAL

Perhaps my favourite role in recent years, however, has been that of theology student. In the early 1990s I had become aware of Regent College, a theological graduate school located on the University of British Columbia campus, when I would drive out from my home in the suburbs to play at coffeehouses in the school's atrium. The first time I wandered into the Regent bookstore, I was astonished to find the works of a great number of theologians, artists and philosophers who meant much to me—writers I had previously encountered haphazardly through my own explorations and never before seen assembled together. I remember scanning the names of authors I had read or wanted to read, my pulse quickening with the realization that the tentative connections I had made were not unique or isolated. There was an entire community making and exploring those connections in rich and expansive ways. I also recognized that I had barely scratched the surface—there were countless authors, titles, ideas and ways of seeing and being yet to be encountered. I resolved to someday attend Regent College.

Almost 20 years later, the longing to study at Regent had not gone away. The escalating opportunities I was being given to write, speak and sing about the things of God intensified my desire to acquire frameworks and, conversely, challenge preconceptions and widen vision. When a church hires me as their retreat speaker or a publisher offers the opportunity to write a book, I am deeply humbled by the trust they are placing in me to influence (even in some small way) the spiritual journeys of other people. I feel a sense of urgency about doing all I can to ensure that whatever ideas are grown in me are planted in the best soil possible. Regent College, it turns out, is an excellent place to cultivate good soil.

Thanks to the ongoing generosity and flexibility of my husband and kids (not to mention some dear friends who helped with tuition fees), I was able to pursue a master's degree at Regent from 2011 to 2014. It was all I had hoped it would be and more. At first, the flood of new ideas, information and paradigms was almost too much to process. But one of the school's fine professors, Dr. Rikk Watts, offered a metaphor in class that I clung to like a lifeline. "Think of yourself as a large fishing net," he told us. "At first, the holes in your net are going to be pretty big, and you're not going to catch everything you wish you could. But you'll still be snagging the biggest, most important fish. Eventually, as you become refined through your education, the holes in your net will become smaller and smaller, and you will catch more and more of what comes your way." His picture helped me relax, trusting I would catch whatever I most needed, and I am happy to report that over time my "net" was refined the way he predicted it would be.

Just like I had to learn that love and connection are the most important parts of a vocation from the stage, Regent showed me that love and connection are the most important parts of learning. I'll never forget the day I met with my first tutorial group. Our professor, Dr. Iwan Russell-

Jones, asked each of us to introduce ourselves and share a bit about our backgrounds. The students in that circle included a judge from Singapore, an American student who had come directly from running an orphanage in Sudan, a corporate lawyer from Washington, DC, an artist from Hong Kong, a worship pastor from Abbotsford, a chemist from the Philippines and, yes, a singer/songwriter/author/speaker from Surrey, BC.

Dr. Russell-Jones looked us over thoughtfully. "We are told in Scripture to 'put on the mind of Christ,'" he said. "But each of us is so tied to our geography and experience that our perspective is profoundly limited. In this room we have a rich variety of ethnic, geographic and vocational backgrounds. Think of all the ways in which we can help each other see the world more like Jesus does. We are meant to do this together."

Regent is an academically robust, challenging environment in which ideas swirl and collide in thrilling ways. But the leaders there are careful to remind all who enter that, much more than information, the goal is transformation. In a forum I attended my first semester, Dr. Bruce Hindmarsh shared some timely leadership advice that had first been spoken a little over a millennium ago by a French Cistercian abbot named Bernard of Clairvaux.

> If, then, you are wise, you will show yourself rather as a reservoir than as a canal. For a canal spreads abroad water as it receives it, but a reservoir waits until it is filled before overflowing, and thus communicates, without loss to itself, its superabundant water...In the Church at the present day we have many canals, few reservoirs.[10]

On my own journey, whatever songs, books, columns, talks or lessons I've offered that have added in any way to God's kingdom have really been the overflow of God's life in me. I suspect you could say the same about your best work, too. May it be true of us that we are not just conduits of good ideas and information but also reservoirs of wisdom and truth in a constant state of being filled to overflowing. May we understand that our work is holy and that our weaknesses might be as important to that

---

[10] Bernard of Clairvaux, *Cantica Canticorum: Eighty-six Sermons on the Song of Solomon*, trans. and ed. Samuel J. Eales (London: Elliot Stock, 1895), 101.

work as our strengths. May we prepare thoroughly, think deeply and train constantly—not to impress but to bless.

And may it all be for love.

---

 Carolyn Arends has released 12 albums and 3 critically acclaimed books. She is also the author of the long-standing "Wrestling With Angels" column in *Christianity Today*. Fifteen of Carolyn's songs have become top-ten radio singles on the Canadian pop and US Christian charts, earning her two Dove Awards, three Juno nominations, and recognition as the West Coast Music Awards' Songwriter of the Year.

Carolyn is the director of education for Renovaré, an organization that encourages and nurtures personal and spiritual renewal through writing, speaking, singing and songwriting. With a degree in psychology and English from Trinity Western University and a master of arts in theological studies from Regent College, she is an adjunct professor at ACTS Seminary, Pacific Life Bible College, and Columbia Bible College, all in British Columbia. Carolyn lives in Surrey, BC, with her husband, Mark, and their children, Benjamin and Bethany.

# Trailblazing

## in Life and Politics

by Deborah Grey

The claw marks were deep and would remain in the door—and the folklore—of that old homestead shack. They told a story of raw terror and the protective nature of a purebred German shepherd named Jireh. It was a bitterly cold night in northeastern Alberta in December 1979. I lay in bed, frozen in fear. I had been teaching at Frog Lake Reserve for some months now and was accustomed to folks from farms or the reserve stopping by for a visit or directions or gas. But never had I heard so much honking, followed by many voices screaming. Jireh leapt up, barking furiously. As car doors opened and closed and the voices got nearer and louder, she lunged at the door. She clamoured to get out and get at them. I could hear her claws gouging the wood. All I could do was picture a headline across tomorrow's newspaper: "Young Single Schoolteacher Murdered Overnight." Panic gripped me.

*Why did I think I could do this? What made me think I could live here alone, so far from any town, and meet the challenges? Why am I, a city kid, trying to convince myself (and others) that I can live in the bush and be completely content?*

At that moment, those questions haunted me. Jireh barked and wanted nothing more than to protect me; I wanted nothing more than to die quickly and not have to suffer. All this noise and seeing my life flash before me took mere seconds.

The screaming stayed loud but suddenly took shape. Was that singing I heard? Impossible! But wait…was that Fritz's voice? Unmistakable! Was that a Christmas carol? Absolutely! A little off-key, words unclear—but sure enough, it was carolers. I got out of what I thought would be my deathbed, calmed Jireh down and opened the door to greet my dear friends Fritz, Jerry and Jeannette, and Liz and Jack. They all tumbled inside, anxious to snuggle up to the cozy wood stove.

When my heart and my stomach traded places and settled down, I told my pals they were lucky to be alive—I had a gun as well as a German shepherd! Then I served coffee, crackers and cheese as I hosted my first-ever shivaree!

As I reflected on the questions I had asked myself in those moments of terror, I clearly recognized the answers. I had always loved the bush and was not only capable of living on my own there but relished it. I loved a challenge and was careful yet not so cautious as to be paranoid. I also knew that God had protected me to that point in my life, and He surely would continue to keep an eye on me, no matter where He wanted me to go and what He wanted me to do.

As one of five kids growing up in a middle-income family in Vancouver, my early life seemed normal and happy. I had three big sisters, and when I was six, we adopted my younger brother, age two. Dad had contracted tuberculosis a few years earlier and then broke his back in a skiing accident after that. He had come from a background of alcoholism, and I wonder if my mother ever secretly worried whether it would surface in him.

These two serious blows to my father were, evidently, more than he could cope with, and he indeed turned to alcohol to escape. Even though he recovered from both health problems and his roofing business prospered again, the seeds of trouble were sown. It became easier to drink for any reason—or no reason. Soon we all learned to read the signs and walk on eggshells when things looked as if they might break loose. It wasn't long before he was spiralling downward, losing his temper and the respect of his family. Some nights he would not come home at all, and we went to bed wondering if he was dead or alive.

One time, on a camping trip, Dad had been drinking and threw me off a raft. I was far from the ladder and screamed and thrashed around in the water. My sisters watched, paralyzed, as they were too far away to reach me. Somehow I made it to the raft and clung on for dear life. At that moment, I made a major life decision: "I will never totally trust that man again." (I also forced myself to swim and later became a lifeguard, addressing that fear head-on!) Also, after seeing the destruction and complete unravelling of such a good person as my father, I made another major life decision: "I will never, ever drink."

The last straw came when Dad sold his business to his long-time secretary and left us. Our livelihood was gone, and so was our father. The pain was devastating, but at least our lives settled down to a state of normalcy. The rules were clear, and Mom was a quiet, steady enforcer of them. She got a job in a lamp store and kept us all fed and together, a remarkable feat in the '60s for a single mom with five kids.

Although I managed to get decent grades in school, I became keenly aware of how teachers and students alike reacted to difficult personal situations. I started noticing kids being picked on and teachers who were the butt of kids' scorn or ridicule. Although I certainly did my fair share of baiting kids and taunting teachers, I did find myself, occasionally, becoming an advocate if I saw what I considered to be injustices being committed against others. For instance, if I saw someone at school being treated unfairly, I would march down to the office and give an account of the incident and declare who I thought to be the guilty party. Also, if I saw kids acting with malice toward a teacher, I would confront them and address the issue. This made me a hero to some, a villain to others. I didn't really care a whole lot—I simply wanted to see justice served.

When I was 13, a friend suggested that I attend summer camp with her. I loved camping and being in the bush. She said Camp Homewood was "a little religious," but not too bad. The water activities and beautiful surroundings would surely make up for it. Camp was wonderful; I loved it. I did find chapel, quiet time (can this be possible for me, even yet?!) and fireside a bit much. But I listened anyway, enjoyed the songs and did well memorizing verses. Some of those verses told me that God loved me no matter what.

My counsellor, Elaine, cared enough about me to listen to my story. She taught me about what it meant to be a Christian: not everything in life is perfect, but God can help you walk through it. I knew that Elaine had a deep faith and that she really believed the stuff she was telling me. Jesus died to forgive the sins of every single person, even me. He rose again and conquered death. I was actually worried about death, because I always wondered if I would see my dad again. The chances of him dying from drinking and driving or freezing to death were certainly above average. So, when Elaine told me that all I had to do was accept God's forgiveness, I was tempted. I knew this was what I wanted, but I worried about what people would say or think of me. On the way home, I longed for the freedom of forgiveness. That night, August 5, 1966, as a 14-year-old girl, I knelt beside my bed and prayed, "Lord, I don't know who You are or what You are. But I am prepared to let You take over the management of my life. I accept Your forgiveness." No lights flashed, no bells rang. I simply knew that my sins were forgiven and I was a new person.

High school went much better for me; I got into much less trouble and had more focus. At age 16, I got my driver's licence and started riding motorcycles immediately. A love affair with wind and winding roads continued for almost 50 years. I graduated with good grades and received the girls' athletic award, the gold pin for drama and the female award of merit (the all-round citizenship award).

I attended Burrard Inlet Bible Institute for three years, getting a good grounding in Christian life and biblical studies. Then I started university at Trinity Western College. I transferred to Edmonton to the University of Alberta to finish my degree and join some friends I had met while on a summer mission project with Operation Mobilization. After finally getting my teaching degree, at age 26, I began teaching at Frog Lake Reserve, in the spring of '79. I had many fabulous experiences there, not the least of which was being taught how to fish with my bare hands by my grade 4 students. I had always believed that a good teacher must also be a good learner. This experience proved that in spades! The kids were thrilled to teach "Grey-Eyes" their craft...and I noticed that they paid more attention to their times tables after they saw me in the role of a learner.

After that spring session and the next year, I landed a job in my area of high school English in Dewberry, Alberta. I loved being part of the community. Every day after school I would go to the post office, the co-op, the bank. The people who worked in all of these places were my students' parents, friends or relatives. Everybody knew everybody, and I quickly got used to the idea of being known by anyone I met on the street. The locals enjoyed studying the new teachers...what we wore, what we drove, how much homework we gave their kids. But they were all extremely friendly, and I regularly had more invitations for coffee than I could accept in any given week.

In the fall of 1988, some friends were gathered at a neighbour's birthday party. The discussion turned to the upcoming election. We had all voted for the Progressive Conservatives, thinking they would get the country's finances back on track, but that had not happened. Deficits were ballooning, and our large contingent of Alberta MPs did not seem to carry much weight in the Mulroney cabinet.

As a Westerner, I felt betrayed in many ways. First, the time zones relegated us to simply playing catch-up on voting day. Majority governments were announced before many of us had even gone to the ballot box. Second, the National Energy Program had devastated Western Canada's oil industry. Billions of dollars were bled out of our economy to Eastern Canada, and the results were catastrophic. Third, Winnipeg had initially won the contract for maintenance work on the fleet of Canadian Forces CF-18 fighter jets. Then, suddenly and with no explanation, the contract was awarded to Montreal. This seemed like another blow levelled at the West. As we discussed and griped about these issues, the topic of the newly formed Reform Party came up. I didn't know much about it, but the name Preston Manning was well respected in Alberta.

I lived in a newly carved-out riding called Beaver River, and the Reform Party had no candidate. My pal Liz suggested that I run! "Don't be ridiculous," I responded. "First, it's September, and I'm up to 'here' with school preparation. Second, I already get enough hassle as a teacher...'too much money, too many holidays.' Why would I sign on for more abuse?"

"But, Deb, we don't have a good candidate, and you would do really well. You can get up and talk, and you aren't afraid to take anyone on. I dare you!" Uh-oh! Those fateful words. I pondered them for mere seconds. I had never backed down from a good dare—ever.

I was sent a party platform and picked it up in the mail on Friday after school as I headed to Edmonton. I was flying to Vancouver for the weekend to attend my brother's wedding. As I sat in the airport reading the material, I discovered that I had always been a reformer, but only now did I realize that someone had put together a platform to enunciate and articulate my feelings! An older gentleman came over and saw the Reform logo. He struck up a conversation and told me he was Gordon Shaw, the vice-chairman of Reform. He had been in Edmonton for campaign meetings with Preston Manning. My heart pounded, wondering at the timing of these "chance" happenings. As a Christian, I believe that God organizes these things. But, no matter what you call it—providence, fate, chance, luck—the common denominator is always the same: the hair on the back of your neck stands up, and the goosebumps arrive immediately!

The writ was dropped on October 5 for a November 21, 1988, election. I was grudgingly granted six weeks of unpaid leave and found my own substitute teacher. I was acclaimed as the candidate on October 12 and was off and running on the campaign trail.

What a ball! We had no clue how to run a campaign, but we had a great team. I learned what the issues were and how to communicate them in bite-size understandable pieces. I knocked on thousands of doors with small teams, attended coffee parties, fall suppers, and so on. The events that I really enjoyed and did well at were the all-candidates' forums.

My campaign team was provided with a complete voters' list from Elections Canada, but we had no idea what to do with it, so I kept it in a box in the back of my vehicle for weight on the winter roads. I also carried around an axe and pounded signs into the freezing ground and, as the campaign wore on, snowbanks.

Free trade became the main issue during that campaign. The debate raged for the full forty-seven-day writ period. On election night, November 21, 1988, the Mulroney Tories ended up with a huge majority and a clear mandate for free trade. No Reformers were elected. I was exhausted. I took Tuesday and Wednesday off school to clean out the campaign office and write thank-you notes.

On Saturday morning, my first chance to collapse and sleep in, the phone awakened me at 9:00 a.m. One of my campaign workers said, "The PC winner [who had been sick during the campaign] just died. Are you ready for a by-election?"

I was already back at school—exhausted, though pleased with our effort. My team was worn out; elections are not for the faint of heart. I felt I could not ask for more time off, so I taught all day and campaigned all night and on weekends. One of the best events of the by-election was attending the PC nomination meeting at Glendon; it was bitterly cold, but there were 4,500 people there. Leadership requires the ability to inspire, and, at 40 below, it takes an extra dose!

My team and I found a bunch of kids and asked them to come outside and give us a hand putting brochures on every windshield. The brochure said, "If you are not happy with the candidate chosen, perhaps you would like to consider Deborah Grey and Reform." This was nervy but paid huge dividends down the road. For years, I had people come up to me saying that they decided to vote for me that very day because I was so gutsy.

We felt a surge in support over the weeks, and my team was very encouraged. On the last weekend of the campaign, we organized a cavalcade. Cars and trucks came from all corners of the riding. We drove around St. Paul, honking and waving banners. The PC candidate's office was on the main drag, and we went past it several times. We only had about 40 or 50 vehicles, and after my first time past, waving and smiling, I ducked each time I went by. This made it look like we had hundreds of cars, going around and around! My team realized that leadership and creativity often go hand in hand.

On by-election night, March 13, 1989, I was getting coffee ready and putting out food trays at our campaign office. A reporter I didn't recognize came in, followed soon after by others I recognized from the national news outlets—CBC, CTV, *Macleans* and Canadian Press. Now I got nervous. They were predicting an upset. What would make a better story, "Another PC Backbencher" or "Reform Party Makes History"?

Not long after the polls closed, I realized that my life had just turned upside down. We had taken 50 percent of the vote! Everybody in our campaign office went crazy. We had all just made Canadian history! As I looked around the office and saw so many people, some of whom I had known and loved for years, some of whom I had just met on the campaign trail, I was in awe. I was about to head to my new classroom.

My first trip to Ottawa was a blur. I was a caucus of one, with nobody to show me the ropes. I learned by trial and error, and the errors were usually on the national news. I had briefings from the clerk and information from the speaker, and I was hiring staff on a wing and a prayer. I was so blessed to find two women who had worked on the Hill for many years, and they remained with me until retirement.

I needed someone to help with the policy and political side, and Preston begged our chief policy officer to move down to help me. He declined the offer, saying that he was taking his master's degree in economics and wanted to complete it. Preston leaned on him some more and impressed upon him how important it was for this greenhorn Reformer to do well. He accepted and said he would come for one year only. Thus, Stephen Harper became my legislative assistant for my first year as a parliamentarian. He was invaluable and got me off to a great start.

My first term was a whirlwind of enormous events, among them the Meech Lake and Charlottetown Accords. These were large constitutional proposals, and I made sure I did everything to let my constituents know what they were all about. I spent all of my weekends at home and traversed the riding during parliamentary recesses. Constituency work in rural ridings is time-consuming, because of the long drives, but always rewarding. I loved meeting people wherever they were and whatever their viewpoints. I often had people visit my riding office who would say they hadn't voted for me but were having trouble with their passport application or Revenue Canada, etc. I always said, "Well, maybe you didn't vote for me, but you're stuck with me! Now, let's see how I can help you." This is what an MP should do, no matter what.

In the fall of 1991, during my first term, I arranged to meet friends in Edmonton for supper, as I was to be at the west end of the riding the next morning. Donna Larson ran our Reform Party office in Edmonton, and she and her husband, Keith, had become good friends of mine. She mentioned that they were going to bring Keith's brother, Lew, along. I was looking forward to an evening with friends without talking "shop" or meeting someone new. Mercifully, Lew was fun to be with and didn't want to talk politics all night!

In the spring of '92, we went out on the paved highway near my place at the lake. I sat in a ditch while he took my Honda 900 CB Custom for his maiden voyage, as it is much easier to ride solo. He gunned the throttle, and away he went with the front wheel coming right off the ground. I was startled and remember thinking, *Oh, I hope he's okay.* It was that very moment that I knew that I was completely in love; otherwise I would have been more worried about my bike than about him!

Kim Campbell became prime minister in June 1993 and started filling in the summer with the BBQ circuit, so we knew the election would probably be in the fall. Lew proposed to me on my forty-first birthday, on July 1, 1993. We were married five weeks later on August 7. We honeymooned in our camper for two weeks, and then we were home barely three weeks before the writ was dropped for an election on October 25, 1993.

Reform rode a wave that saw the PCs decimated and reduced to only two seats nation-wide. The Liberals came up the middle and formed a majority government, with the Bloc Quebecois (separatists) forming Her Majesty's official opposition—one of the most bizarre events in Canadian history, in my opinion. Reform won 52 seats, and I was thrilled to go from "a caucus of one" to "one of a caucus." I served as deputy leader and caucus chairman officially, but unofficially I was den mother and "encourager of the troops." Only two of us had parliamentary experience, and it was no small task to deal with legislation, public life, media training and being away from home all the time. I spent a lot of time counselling and having "teatime" with my colleagues.

In the '97 election, we won 60 seats and became the official opposition. Preston realized that we needed to build our tent bigger and embarked on The United Alternative. This was an attempt to get Conservative-minded voters under one tent, rather than splitting the vote. In 2000, the Canadian Alliance was born, and Preston stepped down to run for the leadership of the Alliance. On March 27, after Preston's recommendation and our caucus's ratification, I became Canada's first-ever female leader of the official opposition!

Over the years, I had done "walkabouts" through our research and communications departments, getting to know the staff. I always enjoyed this and wanted them to know that I appreciated them. Not only that— they were an essential part of our team, and I wanted them to know that. While I served as leader, they fell directly under my authority, and I tried to wander over more often.

My main focus while I served as leader was to keep the whole team together and unified while we were going through the leadership race. I knew that various caucus members would be supporting different candidates, as they had every right to do. But it was essential that we work together regardless of our choices. The whole caucus pulled together, and I was proud of the job we did that spring. The leadership race was not without difficulties in accusations and media focus, as is always the case.

Stockwell Day won the leadership on July 8, 2000. I went to a get-together with Preston's team and looked around the room at the people, many of whom I had known and loved for years. I realized that this was the end of an era, but I knew that we would have to carry on with the mission that we had started so many years earlier. I then went to Stockwell's celebration party to congratulate him. He hugged me and said, "Thank you, Deb. I need you on this team. I really need you." I replied, "I'm here, Stock. I'll do all I can to help you."

He got a seat in the House in a by-election, and then we went into a general election in November 2000. We increased to 66 seats and remained the official opposition. During 2001, we witnessed a series of missteps and blunders in the leader's office, which made it difficult to be supportive as caucus officers. Unbeknownst to each other, Stock's chief of staff, the house leader and I all stepped down from our senior positions on the same day.

Ultimately, a majority of the caucus could not support Stockwell's leadership, and he stepped down, triggering another leadership race, which Stephen Harper won in 2002. After a series of discussions and negotiations, the Conservative Party of Canada was born in 2003, and Stephen won the leadership of it.

I had always had a feeling that if the two parties ever came together I would likely not be a part of it. It was a strange feeling, one I couldn't shake. I had been the flag-bearer, the forerunner and the trailblazer. I wondered for years if that were to be my role in the process. When I announced that I would not seek re-election, I had to answer a barrage of questions about what my "real" agenda and reasons for leaving were. There was nothing hidden or secret. I simply knew in my gut that it was time to move on.

For me, it's sad watching someone go past his or her "best-before" date. I have seen it in politics, academics and the Church. There is nothing worse than seeing a person who's past their prime but hanging on like grim death to something that has slipped away from them. They seem unwilling or unable to admit that it's time to move on to a new chapter in their lives. The saddest thing of all is that, if they refuse to accept a new door graciously, their input lessens and they often become totally ineffective. This seems like a terrible way to go out. I want to learn and grow during each chapter yet be unafraid to let go and move on through the next door.

Is it frightening? Yes. Is it secure? No. Is it comfortable? No. Is it necessary? Yes. If you don't grow and accept challenges, you atrophy in your mind, your soul and your spirit. *If you refuse to renew, you rot.* So many people want to cling to what they have, think they can't do anything else, are afraid to move out of their comfort zone and are afraid to let go of the trapeze they are on now. A trapeze is built in such a way that you can't grab the next bar until you let go of the one you're on. There's no way to hold them both. So, as difficult as it is, you need to let go of the one you're clinging to. When you lose the fire in your belly—for parliament or anything else—it's wrong to keep at it, for yourself and for others. Don't do it. I believe that would lead to a lot of regrets down the road. It could never be worth it, for any reason. We don't get a rehearsal for our career. There's one crack at it. A new challenge is always preferable to regret, in my books.

During the 2004 election, I had the opportunity to introduce Stephen Harper at a huge rally. When he began his speech, he paid me a wonderful compliment. "Ladies and gentlemen, Deb Grey is leaving politics, but not without leaving her mark on the Canadian scene. She has been a pioneer, a warrior and a legend." And to me, that is the way to go out. If I refuse to renew, I will rot.

In the years since my exit from active political life, many doors have opened. I've been busy as a professional speaker with the National Speakers' Bureau. I wander across Canada speaking to various groups about leadership, balancing work and play and maintaining primary relationships. It has been terrific, and Lew says I am still getting paid to talk! Obviously, there's not the same level of political pressure, as I'm able to remain totally non-partisan. That chapter of my life seems so long ago. I truly let it go as soon as I left office. I use examples from my political career, and the stories and principles are generic enough for people in all walks of life to glean tips and tools.

Imagine my surprise when, in 2007, I got a call from the governor general's office asking if I would accept the honour of becoming an officer of the Order of Canada! I thought it was a joke and tried to recognize the voice on the other end of the phone. To this day, I don't know who nominated me or who wrote letters of support for the nomination. But what a thrill it was to be at Rideau Hall having Her Excellency Michaelle Jean put the medal around my neck. I wear the pin proudly every day, even on my leather motorcycle vest!

Lew and I made a major move in 2008, back to the west coast. I had made Alberta my home for over 30 years and really loved it. But winter was becoming less attractive, and I disliked the cold and driving on snowy roads and in blizzards. Lew said one day, "If you thought we had 10 years left to live, where would you want to be?" I immediately responded, "Near the water." I would be happy near any water and assumed we might move to a lake. While visiting my family in Victoria, we drove up-island and travelled to various spots but always returned to Qualicum Beach. The town is quaint, the beach is beautiful, the sunsets, perfect.

In the spring of 2008, we bought a place just a few minutes out of town, and we have settled happily into semi-retirement. We are part of community, with church, coffee and camp friends. We rarely leave the island—mostly for business trips or going to Alberta for family visits. In 2009 one of those business trips took us over to Vancouver for me to receive an honorary doctorate of laws from Trinity Western University. Again, I was totally surprised that anyone remembered my name after I had been out of office for some years. God always has a way of keeping your feet on the ground, as I found out when my brother said to me, "Congratulations, Sis, on becoming Dr. Deb. But, if I get sick, I won't be calling you!" I love being connected this way with Trinity and am proud of their many accomplishments.

In late 2012, I received a call from the prime minister's office. I wasn't terribly surprised, as I thought that maybe Stephen Harper was coming to Vancouver Island and I was being invited to an event nearby. As I prattled away with the young man on the other end of the line, he mentioned that he was the prime minister's director of appointments. I was stunned...and went silent! I had no idea what was coming next. I had been out of office for years and had not lobbied for any political appointments as so many former parliamentarians do.

I was asked to sit on the Security Intelligence Review Committee, the civilian body that reviews CSIS, our spy agency, and makes sure they abide by the law. *Yikes!* I needed to go through all kinds of screening and obtain top-secret security clearance. Also, the CSIS Act states that I needed to be a member of the Queen's Privy Council. Again I found myself at Rideau Hall in April 2013 for a private ceremony with Prime Minister Stephen Harper and His Excellency David Johnston, swearing me into the Privy Council. I was now the Honourable Deborah Grey! It seems that the blessings just keep on coming, even though I have never had any expectations of such lofty honours! I smile at the goodness of God and remember back to my teenage years, when I put my life into God's hands and said, "Here I am...do with me what You please."

My time at SIRC proved to be a tremendous challenge but a fabulous experience, working with a bright, capable team. Only nine months in, I became the interim chair, and the learning curve got even steeper. I went to Ottawa every couple of months and participated in our regular meetings as well as hearing cases of people who had lodged complaints. Without any legal background, I was nervous to be acting as the judge, but I learned the ropes quickly from our legal team. One of the biggest surprises for me was when I walked into the courtroom and everyone was standing. I thought, *Cool, someone important must be coming*. They were standing for me! I quickly learned to smile and say, "Please, be seated."

After just over two years, in April 2015, I was replaced by two very well-qualified people, a bilingual chair who is a retired federal court judge, and a former national security advisor. I was somewhat surprised that I only served two years of my five-year term, but I realized that CSIS and SIRC will only be getting busier, and I am content not to have to travel to Ottawa any more than I had been. It would be easy to be bitter, but I have always chosen to be part of a team as long as the team needs me. I miss the team a lot, but I wish them well as they continue their extremely important work. God always knows what He has in store for me next, and I can't help but smile when I think about it.

If we only talk about leadership but don't live it, then it doesn't count for much. What makes a leader? We must ask, "Who am I? What is my character? Am I the same person at the kitchen table as I am at the office? Where do I want to be and go? When am I a leader? Always? Or only sometimes? Why am I a leader? Because that is the gift I have been given, and I am being untrue to myself and others if I don't use it." If we can't show people that we are leaders, then why would they, why should they, follow us?

I firmly believe that leadership is about thoroughness, thoughtfulness and thankfulness. If we don't exhibit these qualities, we don't deserve to lead. Thoroughness includes doing your homework; a leader should not slack off or be taken by surprise. Too often we see people "coasting," hoping that situations and events will simply "turn out okay." This is unacceptable in today's busy social-media-conscious world. A good leader needs to juggle multiple balls, such as decision-making and paying attention to details.

In decision-making, a good leader needs to gather all the information, weigh the pros and cons, and then decide...and live with the consequences. There is always an exception to the rule, but too often we see people waffle and not make a clear decision. In my political life, I reminded people that it was my name on the lawn sign, not anyone else's. Therefore I needed to be clear and confident in my decision-making.

Regarding details, leaders need to read signs. For example, gestures, silence, sighs and tears will "tell" you things without actually telling you. In my office, I regularly had teatime when I got wind of friction or gossip. It must be nipped in the bud. It's important for a leader to always give people a chance to tell their side of the story, always be fair, always look for a way for everybody to save face and never hope it will just go away. It never does. A boil will always fester.

Thoughtfulness is a necessary quality for a leader. It is essential to build bridges with staff and volunteers; you must always keep an open relationship with staff, yet maintain respect. When my staff came to me with a complaint about a constituent who was particularly rude to them or about me, I would say, "Give me their number, come into my office, and listen while I call them." This was the best way for them to know that a) I actually called the person, b) I defended my staff and c) I called the person's bluff, as they were mostly just being rude and sounding off. My staff always knew that I was on their side and would go to bat for them.

It's always important to look ahead and anticipate needs; for example, if there's new equipment, training or programs that will help, get your staff signed up and prepared for new challenges.

It's also important to understand differences in people. The world is made up of builders versus bashers, copers versus complainers, learners versus lecturers and detailers versus dreamers. We need to maximize our people's strengths. For example, putting a basher or a complainer on the phone to be your public face is not the wisest decision, but they may excel at behind-the-scenes work. Think about your people in your organization. Do you have them in the best place, or job, for their gifting? Do yourself and them a favour; work on this, and you will have a happier, more productive team. You will both be relieved!

As a leader, you must be able to admit when you are wrong. "I blew it. I screwed up. I lost my temper. I made a wrong call. I am sorry." These are the most powerful words a leader can utter. Coupled with this, the genuine ability to celebrate is paramount. Staff will see that not only are you able to apologize; you are also human and enjoy having fun! I suggest that you celebrate big things, little things—any things! I can go berserk over a gorgeous sunset. I can throw a party over the most "insignificant" things. This is because I don't believe anything to be insignificant. Whether my granddaughter climbed higher on the monkey bars or my 80-year-old friend passed her driver's test, it doesn't matter. Both deserve a celebration, either ice cream or coffee at the beach. When each member of my staff had a birthday, they got to pick where we would all go for lunch. This was a terrific investment for me, as their boss. Besides the enjoyment of every moment of the celebration, the reciprocation was having a loyal and loving staff. I would do it again in a heartbeat.

I also believe in the power of laughter, mostly at myself. I participated in TV skits on *This Hour Has 22 Minutes* and *Royal Canadian Air Farce* during my years in public life. Again, besides being such a ridiculous amount of fun, it sent the message that I didn't ever take myself too seriously.

And at the end of the day, thankfulness must reign. Do you ever just stop and ponder what a great job you have? Many days, while teaching and while serving in elected life, I thought to myself, *And I get paid for this?* If you hate it, leave it—you aren't fooling anyone.

Be fair to yourself and your colleagues. Realize that people want to work together and be part of a team. As a leader, don't only say "thank you" but also show your thankfulness. Avoid workplace romances. We often hear about this, but it is an easy thing to slip into. These often have unhappy endings. It puts co-workers in an awkward spot, and if the relationship goes sour, it can destroy an entire office. People can choose sides, and the atmosphere becomes deadly poisonous.

After thinking about all these qualities and attributes, ask yourself, "Am I the kind of boss I would like to have?" Your answer might be very telling and also give you the opportunity to change. Maria Robinson, an American author and child expert, said, "Nobody can go back and start a new beginning, but anyone can start today and make a new ending." I love what this captures. Yesterday is gone, but you have today, so grab the chance while you have it!

## FINAL WORD

Nellie McClung, one of the "Famous Five" who succeeded at having women recognized as "persons" in 1929, was a leader who didn't back down. I have loved and lived one of her most famous quotes (and used it as the title of my autobiography in 2004): "Never retreat, never explain, never apologize—get the thing done and let them howl."[11] So much time is wasted and frittered away while we dither, wondering what to do. Start today! Make your new ending! Never retreat!

When I had just made Canadian history and my life had turned upside down, I had the extraordinary opportunity of meeting Douglas Campbell, one of the original Progressives, who was elected to Parliament in 1922 and then went on to become Manitoba's premier in 1948. He was 93 at this time, and he told me stories of Agnes Macphail, another Progressive and the first-ever woman member of Parliament to sit in the House of Commons, also elected in 1922. He mentioned how ironic it was that Agnes and I did not represent the mainstream parties and that we were women, starting something new. I was excited but felt somewhat unworthy to be walking in her footsteps. I thought about my responsibility to lead by example and "reproduce" myself in others, especially younger women who would watch my career and be encouraged to step out of their own shadow and take a dare, whatever that looked like.

Douglas Campbell passed the torch from the original populist movements to the new generation of Reform. Surely bridges have been built from the past to the present, and he was the living embodiment of it, right before my eyes. He quoted, from memory, this poem by (Miss) Will Allen Dromgoole:

## The Bridge Builder

An old man going a lone highway,
Came, at the evening cold and gray,
To a chasm vast and deep and wide.
Through which was flowing a sullen tide.

---

[11] Nellie McClung, quoted in Veronica Strong-Boag, introduction to *In Times Like These*, by Nellie L. McClung (Toronto: University of Toronto, 1972), vii.

The old man crossed in the twilight dim,
That sullen stream had no fear for him;
But he turned when safe on the other side
And built a bridge to span the tide.
"Old man," said a fellow pilgrim near,
"You are wasting your strength in building here;
Your journey will end with the ending day,
You never again will pass this way;
You've crossed the chasm, deep and wide,
Why build this bridge at evening tide?"
The builder lifted his old gray head;
"Good friend, in the path I have come," he said,
"There followed after me to-day
A youth whose feet must pass this way.
This chasm that has been naught to me
To that fair-haired youth may a pitfall be;
He, too, must cross in the twilight dim;
Good friend, I am building this bridge for him."[12]

As Douglas Campbell built bridges for me, my mission is to build bridges for others.

---

 The Honourable Deborah Grey was raised in Vancouver, BC, where she attended Trinity Western University. She later earned a bachelor of arts and education at the University of Alberta. After teaching school in northeastern Alberta for ten years, Deborah made Canadian history in 1989 as Canada's first-ever Reform Party member of Parliament. She sat in the House of Commons until 2004. Deborah is the recipient of an honorary doctorate of laws from Trinity Western University and Alberta's Centennial Medal.

---

[12] Will Allen Dromgoole, "The Bridge Builder," in *Father: An Anthology of Verse* (Boston: EP Dutton & Company, 1931). Public domain.

Deborah is a professional speaker, an active volunteer with several charitable organizations, an officer of the Order of Canada and a member of the Queen's Privy Council. She and her husband, Lewis, are happily semi-retired in Qualicum Beach, BC, and are often seen riding their matching Honda Valkyrie motorcycles.

# *Pursuing*

## a World View of Poverty and Social Justice

by M. Christine MacMillan

### LEADERSHIP AS A CHOICE

The first footsteps of leaders are tentative. I should know. Looking back on my first positions of leadership, my doubts and fears made me reticent. I tiptoed into my first assignments. Still, those first steps not only left an imprint on the person I grew up to be, but they also created a pattern for my leadership that kept reappearing as I embraced increasing responsibilities.

I was born in Montreal and attended Sunday school with my parents. The adult leaders at church encouraged the children to participate in the activities. And so at three years old I found myself walking in a circle with my peers to the rhythm of "Jesus Loves Me," directed by the ping of a triangle sounding from my little hands. Could I pass the test of multi-tasking?

My young mind was stressed—not about the task itself but because I was being watched by the adults. I accomplished the activity, but my mind was gripped with fear.

I headed for the closest door and ended up in the hallway corridor—unlit, pitch-black—with tears coming down my rosy cheeks. In that moment I had an encounter with the demands of leadership. Always shy (even to this day), I began to realize its challenges. Leadership is choosing a will far greater than our own inclinations and comfort levels.

The "Jesus Loves Me" kid has explored dimensions of that song beyond the obvious. As leaders, we face many challenges in allowing Jesus' love to shape, bend and motivate our leadership. My leadership journey has been marked by choices, choices and more choices, shaped within the richness of struggle.

## EMERGING LEADERSHIP

As I grew older—and, from outward appearances, learned how to overcome my shyness—I became a leader in areas of my strength and comfort. After high school, I studied social work. This led to a position with Toronto's welfare department. Home visits to clients pushed open new doors that allowed me to view poverty and shattered relationships up close.

I enjoyed this work, and God challenged me to engage with the complexities of the lives I encountered. I wondered about the upcoming generation born into these situations and how they would live. Passionate about creating a solution, I approached my supervisor about an experiment that was eventually approved: I moved out of the regional office to the housing estate to be on-site and available to my clients.

My choice to stand in the gap for my clients in the midst of their struggles went beyond the boundaries of what was expected of me. At one point, I was able to convince a local school principal to open the school gym on a weekly basis to provide a place where people could go for recreation in a caring environment. I took on the responsibilities of running the program and protecting the property. Love was not restricted to my timeline, job description or calculated lifestyle. I led from intention of heart, knowing that expertise would follow.

I kept up socially at that time with friends who were frustrated with the status quo of the church as a shelter from the evil world. We believed in taking the gospel outside of the church walls, so we established a drama company of university-age promising writers and actors and developed scripts of modern-day parables, which made it to the big-time commercial world of theatre. Our theatre company was known in newspaper reviews for its gospel creed and class act on stage. This was hip, intellectual and creative—a gospel Beatlemania, you might say. For me it was a time of exhilaration.

It was also a time of doubt. Being cutting edge was not enough. I felt the need to face the dark corridors of my own humanity. I needed to be willing to see issues of conflict and failure as leverage points for achieving new heights. My evangelistic fervour needed the balance of inward formation—the kind that recognizes that evangelical lifestyles and teaching would be hollow if my words were not rooted in a character that mirrored those words.

## MAKING IDEAS REALITY

A holiday to Bermuda exposed a gnawing call on my life. While visiting close family in Bermuda, I attended a Salvation Army music camp with my cousins. The guest leaders, Majors Margaret and David Hammond, hailed from Toronto. On the pristine Bermuda beaches, we discussed their ministry. They had been praying for opportunities to reach their local neighbourhoods back home. Knowing my social work background, they asked if I had any ideas. I did!

That conversation led to an invitation to join their Salvation Army church staff. The salary would mean a 50 percent pay cut from what I was making with the government, and such a position had not been tried before in the Salvation Army in Canada. It sounded experimental and intriguing.

The contract was drawn up, and, only a few days later, the community newspaper sent their reporter and photojournalist to the church in Toronto to interview me. Later that week, a full two-page centre spread and front cover picture of yours truly hit the congregation, causing some trepidation. The photos were set up to provoke a little controversy as the headline read, "Miniskirted Chris helps change Army's bugles-and-bonnets image." I was asked to sit on a desk for a pose that lent itself to the title. Was my leadership challenging the mould of a well-uniformed Sally Ann image?

I went to work to fill the new church building with the marginalized of the community, from children to the lonely elderly. The place was bustling, and the congregation was watching. Slowly some volunteers emerged from the comfortable pews.

Leaders plant "idea" seeds. Some of these seeds grow to be solid concepts with great possibilities. Often a leader's ideas never bear fruit until that leader works hard to develop those ideas so that others can see the idea "in the flesh." It can be a lonely task to develop an idea, especially if the initial reaction to it is negative. It can also be a challenge to go from an idea to an actual detailed plan.

In my case, the Salvation Army did have social services, but they were operational outside the walls of the church more than inside. I was blessed because Majors Margaret and David Hammond heard my ideas and could conceptualize them. How important it is for a leader to have support! I needed their support if I was to make my ideas a reality in our community. Even though leadership can be lonely, we should not be alone on our journey. Find someone who believes in your vision and will support your ideas.

## GOD, MY HEADHUNTER!

Organizations vary in their entry points of leadership. Education, CVs and a savvy job interview are the usual steps for career advancement. Headhunters may also knock on your door as your reputation makes you sought after. But what if God is your headhunter?

While working in my role at the church, I was asked to attend a Salvation Army discernment weekend with several other young people. The weekend was intended to be a time of prayer and reflection to discern whether God was calling us to enter seminary for full-time ordained ministry.

The weekend was attended by six other young people from our church and ended with our return to our local church for the Sunday evening service. Within our service structure, opportunities are sometimes given for testimonies. All six stood one by one and shared their intent to become ordained within the Salvation Army. Number seven was still sitting in the pew. I slowly stood to my feet and said with a quiet voice, "I guess I am going to the training college." I could see my pastors expressing both surprise and joy. After all, it was only a few months since miniskirted Chris had hit the headlines.

The words coming from my mouth that day were not confident, assured or even peaceful. I had some idea what the covenant commitment required by the Salvation Army would entail. In all likelihood it would include a single lifestyle, although marriage could take place with another ordained "officer." The Salvation Army would determine my career path, telling me what my role would be, where I would serve and where I would live, right down to a home address with furnishings and decor owned by the Salvation Army. Moving locations on a regular basis would be part of the equation. Comfort levels of personal choices would be laid on the line.

Following my training, I stood on a public platform before a packed audience in Massey Hall, Toronto, to receive my first appointment. I was in my twenties, and I didn't know yet what that appointment would be. In my new Salvation Army uniform, bonnet and all—it was not a miniskirted Chris that everyone saw—and with the rousing tones of our Salvation Army band setting the atmosphere of victory, I was deemed to be ready for service.

This was not the path that I would have naturally chosen. It was a path I was not too sure about. But it was the path God designed for me. Leadership is often about letting God direct one's paths. Does it always make sense? Not at first, but as I trusted God and moved forward, I began to see how God's grand design for my life was taking shape.

## PRACTICING RELATIONAL LEADERSHIP VALUES

Only a few months after I graduated from the Salvation Army Training College in Toronto, I was appointed to Vancouver, Canada, as the assistant administrator of Homestead, a treatment centre for women with addictions. The centre was located in a very large house and provided for 11 residential clients plus a two-bed detox centre, which, at that time, was a rare service in the Vancouver. My theological and ministry training developed my professionalism, compassion and spiritual relevance. But my assignment required skills beyond social work experience, so I eventually received certification as an International Certified Alcohol and Drug Counsellor.

My influence, spreading throughout the Christian community, resulted in a network of support for women experiencing addictions. I began to be called upon by the wider secular community of professionals on issues relating to spirituality. The province of BC was a place where witchcraft settings were affecting individuals with trauma and addiction-related issues. Some cases of abuse, including ritualistic murder, had landed in the courts. I was called upon as an expert because of my combined skills as an addiction professional and minister.

Communicating a leadership style beyond what came naturally to me taught me to practice relational leadership values. At times I was viewed by others in the secular realm as the "confessor" for a host of personal and private issues that other professionals were experiencing. For me to be successful, it was also necessary to build relationships with the members of the ministerial of the Downtown Eastside. In the Salvation Army, collaboration is not one of our strong suits. I needed to find ways to build trust and find points of connection. For me, this was our shared vision to impact the community.

Ministering at the treatment centre also challenged me to lead by building relationships. I observed a sea of humanity struggling in the vulnerability of Vancouver's Downtown Eastside. The only way for me to truly impact these lives was to build rapport with them and to engage in their lives. I continued to conduct my ministry on the front lines—on streets that oozed with violence, addiction, prostitution and mental illness, streets filled with people who embraced despair.

At first, my immediate intervention motto was "Rescue the perishing, care for the dying." Over those 15 years, my general desire to care was translated into names, stories and personalities, all linked to tears and laughter shared under the night light of the street. My level of fatigue in those late and long hours was high, but I was sustained by a community that welcomed my effort. I was forming a relationship with Jesus that went far beyond my seminary classroom instruction. I saw a Jesus and felt a Jesus whose care for others demonstrated a flexibility of spirit while challenging the labels of containment. I was drawn to the response of Jesus when He said, when under criticism for breaking the barriers of the status quo, "I desire mercy, and not sacrifice" (Matthew 12:7).

Eugene Peterson laments how the church can sometimes be too far removed from the people.

> Ecclesiastical affairs require armies of ordained men and women to keep the wheels turning. Instead of putting us on the front lines of reconciling love for the world, ordination has conscripted us into jobs and agendas that effectively remove us from the very plight that is the reason for our ordination.[13]

---

[13] Marva Dawn, Eugene Peterson, and Peter Santucci, *The Unnecessary Pastor: Rediscovering the Call* (Grand Rapids: Eerdmans, 2000), 17.

I had opportunities for further education, but I decided to stay in Vancouver. Interacting with the lives of those in my community in a sense was its own form of education. For leaders, very real relationships like those I developed on the streets can develop our leadership abilities and character as much—or even more—than the classroom can.

## TRANSFORMATIONAL LEADERSHIP

In Matthew 12, we read about Jesus and His disciples walking through grain fields on the Sabbath. His disciples were breaking off heads of wheat and eating the grain. Then, on the way to the synagogue, Jesus noticed a man with a deformed hand and healed him. Picking wheat to eat and healing a disability sound like harmless actions to us, but to the Pharisees, these actions violated the law to remember the Sabbath day and keep it holy. Legalistic perspectives of working on the Sabbath were pitted against Jesus' call to proclaim the kingdom of God by feeding the hungry and healing the sick. Jesus replied to His critics, "I desire mercy, and not sacrifice." Like Jesus, there were times when I faced criticism when choosing to cross the boundaries of tradition, respectability and "protocol" for the greater good. This story encouraged me to keep choosing mercy over reputation when I needed to make difficult decisions in my leadership.

However, the pursuit of mercy can take its toll. The work of serving the suffering has many obstacles that can cause stress and fatigue; lack of funding, potential lawsuits and ineffective outcomes are just a few. Compassion fatigue can also include the fear of being criticized for not meeting the high standards demanded of NGOs. All of these stress factors can tempt one to parade one's sacrifice of hard work to an audience of well-wishers—but that is not the attitude that Christ requires of us. Jesus said, "But when you do merciful deeds, don't let your left hand know what your right hand does" (Matthew 6:3, WEB). Stories of past leaders in the Salvation Army remind me of the goal of self-abandonment for a greater cause. As leaders, we continually grapple with our need for recognition. We sometimes cheapen our power by our overwhelming need to feel valued, significant and worthy and do so at the cost of foregoing the ethic of self-abandonment.

## DEVELOPING STRATEGIC PERSPECTIVES

Fifteen years of building services in Vancouver came to an end. I was appointed to London, England, where the Salvation Army had been working with a university to undertake a major study on homelessness, which would inform the government, NGOs, the global community and citizens at large. With all my experience, it would be so easy to stay at a distance, settle down and simply advise from my office. This is perhaps a trap we all face: the temptation of staying comfortable. But we cannot lead unless we are close to the people to whom we minister.

How could I understand homelessness in the UK unless I experienced it from the front lines? I asked if I could move into the East End of London, where the Salvation Army started in 1865. I lived in a women's hostel called Hopetown for a number of months and undertook my own research project in assessing the needs of the residents, who were being housed but faced deeper inner issues.

Five years in the United Kingdom gave me the opportunity to develop big-picture strategies that bridged front-line experience and a macro style of leadership. Navigating your own setting is one thing, but trying to get others on board is difficult. As we developed a paradigm that gave the clients of our homelessness services a more participative role, I asked myself, was my leadership style reflective, absorbing and consultative? Was I engaging without having to be in charge?

The opportunity to sit with representatives of government and the Prince Charles Trust, as well as the dean of Westminster Abbey, enlarged my strategic perspective, influence and questions. I recall the personal invitation that came from the secretary of the Prince Charles Trust. A private meeting was being set up with 25 key stakeholders who could both inform the prince and listen to his response on social engagement.

I was told in advance that a speech would be given and then Prince Charles would turn to me and say, "Christine, what did you think of that?"

"Okay," I said to the organizer. "When do I get a copy of the talk so that I can formulate my thoughts?"

"You don't," he responded. "I want it to be extemporaneous. You can do it; I have heard you before." Well, the tension was mounting!

The talk was given, and, sure enough, Charles turned his head and said, "Christine, what do you think?" I shared my insights naturally and simply. At the end of the meeting, Prince Charles turned his head towards me again and said, "We must never forget what Christine said at the beginning of this meeting." I realized in that moment that I had spoken only what I truly thought and had left the need for impressing behind.

God has a way of grounding us in a humility that is not our own. I was grateful for the opportunity to meet such influential people. And, believe me, preparing for such events requires more than our words. Our surrender to the greater good leaves ego-tripping at home, but not without a preparation of heart, mind and spirit.

## FOLLOWING GOD'S LEAD

The season of ministry in London came to an end when I returned to territorial headquarters in Toronto, Canada, as director of program with the social services department. The next move brought me to the divisional office in Kingston, Ontario, where I was groomed to be the divisional commander (bishop) in a few short months. I had just started the position when a phone call came, announcing an appointment for me in Sydney, Australia, as territorial secretary for program. A few weeks later, I was bound for the "Land Down Under."

God then brought me to Papua New Guinea as the new territorial commander. This was an unusual appointment for a single white woman! After all, Papua New Guinea was a patriarchal society, and there were certainly no female denominational leaders. Some questions were certainly raised around the wisdom of a single woman Salvation Army officer taking the lead.

Another phone call from the general and, yes, a new assignment. I returned home to be the territorial commander of the Canada and Bermuda Territory. How would I manage this transition in my leadership context? Being territorial commander of the Canada and Bermuda Territory would prove to be very different from the kind of leadership I exercised as territorial commander in Papua New Guinea, where I could practice my relational style of leadership on a daily basis.

Delivering social services that ranged from street ministry to full-scale hospitals, the Salvation Army was the highest provider of social services next to the government. Giving direction to such a large corporation, I was asked on more than one occasion to outline my vision for the territory. Such a question pushed me in the direction of becoming a leader soloist— all things to all people. This grated on my conscience. To hear from the constituency and understand the context of Canadian and Bermudian society needed time and reflection. My first task, undertaken through a rigorous travel schedule and multiple engagements, was listening, listening and more listening.

Following these exploration travels, I went away to be on my own for two days to pray, think and return with a draft vision. The vision started off with the statement "We are a territory in ongoing conversation," followed by a set of objectives. As an overriding statement, my starting point signalled that I as a leader regarded the participation of others as credible, responsible and valuable. I was confident that this approach would create followers who would hold a stake in the objectives of the vision. My inner circle, the cabinet, was invaluable as a team and loyal in the best sense by wanting the essentials for the Salvation Army's mission in building the kingdom of God.

Salvation Army generals can pick up the phone and inform senior leaders of their next appointment at any time, and sure enough a phone call came from General Clifton. But this invitation would be my last. I was to pioneer a new department of the international headquarters—the International Social Justice Commission. The commission's mandate was to help the Salvation Army integrate its historic mission—to serve among the poor and invite them into following Jesus Christ—with God's call to address large-scale injustice in the world. The commission would be based in New York City to take advantage of the proximity to the United Nations head offices.

I confess that the learning curve was steep. However, learning about the afflictions of an unjust world challenged me and my colleagues, Dr. James Read and Dr. Don Posterski, to stand up and speak out in the powerful places of our world. We discovered that it was not enough to confine our compassion to traditional church ministries. At times we identified with the prophets of Scripture because we were perceived as unpopular messengers of depth, challenge and even controversy. This led the three of us to write a book called *When Justice Is the Measure*, which provided biblical and experiential insights into the global injustices that we were grappling with.

We were exchanging our fear of failure for a freedom to risk failure. We recognized the need to develop skills to effectively advocate with government leaders, policy makers and the secular world in general.

Praying invocations at public events would not be enough. Our drive to focus more outwardly and less inwardly kept the Micah 6:8 question before us and the Salvation Army: "What does the LORD require of you...?" I was sensing within myself a need to work harder and engage in deeper commitment—activities that could have lapsed into simply praying more and preaching louder.

The world of suffering and injustice is traumatic, overwhelming and confusing. I was travelling 100,000 miles a year in this new role, sitting on planes more than sitting at home and in the office. Was I attending to my need for reflection? After all, we insisted that our interns meet with me regularly for spiritual formation. How was I being responsible and accountable for my own well-being?

I sought out a spiritual director. Sister Alice Feeley, a woman of great patience, insight and faith, filled that role and provided a safe environment for me to unpack my leadership role, rank and expectations. Looking back I'm so grateful that I allowed myself to trust Alice. She helped me to discern my own convictions and define my leadership style in an atmosphere of trust. These new discoveries were grounded in a deeper understanding of my personal salvation in Jesus Christ and the unconditional love of God.

Five years after establishing the International Social Justice Commission, I concluded my Salvation Army formal service at an honourable age of retirement. Little did I know that the phones would start ringing from organizations outside of the Salvation Army with offers I could not then imagine.

Two substantial work requests came my way following my retirement. My good friend Lorna Dueck, then president and executive producer of Media Voice Generation and a weekly television show, *Context with Lorna Dueck*, offered me a position at her offices in the CBC building in downtown Toronto. I accepted the offer and was able to help develop a paradigm shift of leadership infrastructure within Media Voice Generation.

Also, Geoff Tunnicliffe, secretary general of the World Evangelical Alliance (WEA) in New York City, asked if I would serve as senior advisor for social justice (I was already chairing their task force on human trafficking). God has opened the door for me to work with WEA as director of public engagement, my current role, helping to articulate and engage the voice of the Church at the United Nations and in settings of worldwide significance, as well as the constituency of 600 million that the WEA represents.

ᄋᎧ

Throughout these later leadership years, I grew to appreciate the power of several basic leadership principles that I want to share with you.

To make a true and lasting impact, to spiritually challenge the hearts of our people, I needed to attend to my own formation as a leader and disciple. I needed to share my heart as leader. Leadership required that I go beyond my position to embrace a *lifestyle* of leadership. As we mature as leaders, we need to remember that we are models and inspirations to others at all times. To lead is to accept God's call and design for our life. And God's call is not restrained to a 9 a.m. to 5 p.m. routine.

Humility and self-abandonment are needed at all times. Will you make a big impact on others? Absolutely. But remember to give God glory and thanksgiving for the transformation that is brought about through your ministry. God is *your* leader. Follow His lead. Be willing to step out of your comfort zone, to be stretched, to be moulded. Be willing to learn and have a teachable spirit so that God can train you to meet every challenge.

Relationships are key. Be a relational leader. Think of ways to collaborate with others to bring about a greater impact in your community. Be involved in your community and in the lives of the people in your ministry.

Finally, let Jesus be your inspiration, and learn from the way that Jesus valued and cared for others. Grow in your faith. Trust God at all times.

## POSTSCRIPT

The leadership principles that I can see working through my life are apprehended from a vantage point I didn't anticipate when I said yes to the request to write a chapter in this book. Since December 2015, I have been living with cancer, experiencing new and at times overwhelming feelings of weakness and isolation.

Over the eight months since my diagnosis I have been continually reminded of the suffering that I have encountered in so many people in my leadership roles. Could it be that living with cancer has not changed the kind of leader that I am but has actually strengthened me to be the leader

God made me to be? It seems that my voice among those who serve among suffering people is amplified through my personal experience of suffering.

The most precious gift of all is knowing Jesus more deeply as "a man of sorrows and acquainted with grief" (Isaiah 53:3). He truly experiences with me my horror, deep distress and anguish.

Leadership in one's life is not restricted to formal positions. I'm forever grateful to the leadership given by a medical professional who looked beyond a disease into my heart and mind. Friends and family have been the glue that has me sticking to a new normal while continuing my official role with the WEA through virtual means until I can regain the capacity to travel.

As I write this story of my leadership journey, the cancer chapter is not yet complete. While still in the midst of treatment, I am given over to the hope that my Saviour leader never gives up on accompanying me. He will lead me into new discoveries and into everlasting life. In all this God continues to give me life and opportunities to serve—I'm still listening.

Here I am Lord. Is it I Lord?
I have heard you calling in the night.[14]

---

An inspiring and effective advocate of social justice, Commissioner Christine MacMillan served as a Salvation Army officer, holding appointments in six countries: Canada, Bermuda, Australia, England, Papua New Guinea, and the United States. In 2007, Christine became the founding director of the Salvation Army International Social Justice Committee, and following her retirement in 2012, she was invited to work at the World Evangelical Alliance, where she now serves as the director of public engagement. Working with the United Nations and others in the international community, Christine identifies key global social issues and implements strategies and responses on behalf of the WEA. She is a frequent speaker and the author of *When Justice Is the Measure*.

---

[14] Lyrics to "Here I Am, Lord," by Daniel L. Schutte (OCP Publications, 1981).

# *Setting*

## the Course for Freedom

by Janet Epp Buckingham

*"Have I not commanded you? Be strong and courageous. Do not be frightened, and do not be dismayed, for the LORD your God is with you wherever you go."* (Joshua 1:9)

Little does one know what life will bring or how the leadership development journey will unfold. I have often reflected on Jeremiah 29:11: "For I know the plans I have for you, declares the LORD, plans for welfare and not for evil, to give you a future and a hope." We know instinctively that God has a plan and purpose for our lives. We hold tightly to His promise that He will be with us. Yet the journey is unknown. By working through challenges, the unexpected, and the twists and turns of life, we can gradually align ourselves with God's plan and purposes. My leadership journey included lessons on character building, finding balance, learning to forgive and facing what seemed at the time "larger-than-life" growth challenges.

## GOOD LEADERSHIP BEGINS WITH GOOD ROLE MODELS

Good leadership does not grow out of a vacuum. Every leader that I know has been influenced by someone who modeled the core aspects of leadership: character, integrity and a strong work ethic. For me, that person was my father. Dad had a strong ethical framework and was a hard worker. His favourite saying was "If a thing is worth doing, it is worth doing well." As a busy corporate executive, Dad spent many years entrusted with the finances of large corporations, but it never occurred to him to act unethically. Dad's integrity was known throughout his company. In fact, after my father's death, one of his former colleagues said the ethical failures at Enron and Worldcom would not have happened if my father had been there. The results would have been very different.

I was definitely a "daddy's girl" and quickly absorbed Dad's values, which helped to shape the foundations of my leadership. But Dad also helped me to see my own unique strengths. I was the only extrovert in a family of introverts. My family teased me, telling me that I talked too much. However, because my father was a corporate executive and we moved a great deal for this work, my "talking too much" gave me an advantage. I did not find it difficult to make new friends and find my way in new schools. As life unfolded, my ease in talking gave me the ability to be flexible and adapt quickly to new situations. While I do not believe it is necessary to be an extrovert to be a leader, communicating effectively has been a gift to me and instrumental in my advocacy. Being the only extrovert in my family drew me out and has become one of my strengths in my work.

While clerking for judges at the Federal Court of Canada, I began dating Don, a man from Saskatchewan who modeled the same values as my father—character, integrity and a strong work ethic. Don eventually became my husband and an instrumental partner in my development as a leader. Little did I know how well-suited Don would be to me. He is the most egalitarian man I know and has always treated me as an equal and supported my hopes, dreams and aspirations. Don is very non-confrontational, which balances my take-charge personality. Like iron sharpening iron, opposites shape character, if the right attitude is taken. Don has a strong gift of encouragement, which helped me to believe in my God-given gifts and abilities even when I doubted them. It is a huge blessing to have a husband who affirms God's calling on my life and supports me no matter what! Don was God's choice for me.

## EFFECTIVE LEADERS PRACTICE SELF-CARE

My learning curve as a young woman finding herself was steep. Like many in leadership, I had a tendency to take on too many responsibilities. And like many in leadership, I too had to learn the painful lesson that comes with burnout. We all have an internal emotional reserve that needs to be refuelled or we will run on empty. I ran on empty!

In my last year of high school I was asked to produce the school musical. It was a monumental responsibility that required coordinating many volunteers, all of them high school students. Amid this project, I was nominated to participate in the Forum for Young Canadians in Ottawa. This was in addition to a heavy academic load.

At the end of the year I crashed. Much of the exam period was spent in bed. I was able to do little more than crawl out for meals and then go back to sleep. This was my first experience of burnout.

Listening to your body is imperative to finding a proper balance between work and rest. Understanding what energizes you and what depletes you is equally imperative. Working in your giftings, calling and abilities always gives you energy. Depletion happens when you try to function too long in your non-gifted areas.

Finding a healthy balance does not happen overnight. It's a gradual learning experience but one that will prevent burnout for the leader who has drive and passion. Recovery for me came slowly, but it gave me valuable self-care and soul-care lessons for the future.

## BUILDING AND DEVELOPING RELATIONSHIPS IS THE HEART OF LEADERSHIP

Being the extrovert that I was, leadership came naturally to me. But I learned early on that it is one thing to give visionary leadership and it is quite another to lead people. I had some painful lessons in learning how to work with people and really love them!

Throughout my university years I held a number of leadership positions, like vice president of the history club and law representative on Dalhousie Student Union. These were honourable positions that gave me a sense of pride and accomplishment. My American history professor lauded me for putting out the first history journal in several years. When I set my mind to doing something, I made sure that I accomplished it. In those days, I didn't care if I ruffled some feathers while achieving my goals. My husband refers to this as my tendency to act as "a beaver on a bulldozer." I did not realize it, but my approach drove people away.

Painful lessons came out of this time. While leadership involves getting things done, building and developing relationships are critical and reflect the heart of the leader. Leaders are always trying to find that delicate balance between two conflicting activities—reaching a goal and responding correctly to people.

Investing in people and building life-empowering relationships are at the heart and core of leadership. Gaining greater influence always comes back to our relationships with people. It's a constant learning curve for leaders because of the complexity of human nature. Leaders learn to love people.

An important aspect of building and developing relationships is recognizing the need of building community, team spirit and a sense of belonging. During law school, I lived with four other Christian students in a "community house." All of us were involved in student ministry in some way and were deliberate about being a community. This experience taught me important lessons about being a team player and taking part in something bigger than myself. Much later, in leadership positions, I was intentional to connect regularly with those on my team to ensure that their needs were being met.

In these years, I learned that people need to *belong*. It's an inherent need that helps people to grow and thrive. Leaders are not exempt. We are wired to love, to be loved and to belong. Belonging is a soul-need that gives us worth, value, a sense of inner shelter and peace.

## A DEEP TRUST IN GOD IS CRITICAL FOR CHRISTIAN LEADERS

Change is written into life. Life is continually handing us changes. How we respond to change has greater consequences than we realize.

Don and I moved from Halifax to England in September 1989 for Don to complete grad school at Cambridge University. What a year it was! The Berlin Wall came down that fall, and South Africa began the transition from apartheid to full participation of all races. It was also the most difficult year of our married life. As a developing leader, I learned to cope with the changes around us and within us. We were being stretched and had to adjust. Before we left Canada, we were practising lawyers at law firms, jobs with decent salaries and a certain amount of prestige. I was not prepared for the change back to student life. Nor was Don. Yet this period of change and adjustment inspired the most growth.

I learned in Cambridge that we were divinely directed. Even in the midst of change, frustration and tough tests, God surprised me. Within a week of arriving, I had two great opportunities. The first was to study at Romsey House, a Bible college. The second was to volunteer with the Jubilee Centre, a Christian public policy think tank. Studying the Bible and theology at Romsey House deepened my spiritual life. The Jubilee Centre gave me my life calling. I worked on a project on South Africa. The centre held two symposia during my year there, one on federalism and another on human rights, both of which were in my areas of expertise. The centre's director, Michael Schluter, gave me the opportunity to give my first academic paper on comparative federalism. I was both terrified and excited. During the second symposium, the African National Congress (ANC) was unbanned as an organization, allowing it as a legal organization. It was very moving to sit across the table from a black South African member of the ANC who had not been able to return to his country for more than 20 years.

Through these experiences, God taught me that I can trust in Him, even in the midst of change and uncertainty. God used Romsey House and the Jubilee Centre to draw out more of my potential and further solidify my calling. It gave me a much clearer focus on the direction my life would take. I became alive in the area of Christian public policy. I didn't know it, but God was setting me up in a season of change towards Christian public policy.

Often in life and in leadership there is a test within a test. I was doubly tested when I was pregnant with my first son. My life became very complicated and almost out of control. I had planned to take the allotted six months off for maternity leave from my role as executive director for Eastern Canada for the Christian Legal Fellowship (CLF) after Ben was born, but that was not to be. The executive director for Western Canada, who was supposed to cover for me, took the time off instead. His law partnership dissolved, and he needed to rebuild his legal practice. Apparently that was more demanding than having a newborn! I was frustrated and felt overwhelmed, particularly as the board of directors of CLF didn't even discuss possible alternatives. I felt that I had no option but to carry on and even expand my work, with only a week of leave.

Fortunately, I had family and friends who came to the rescue and babysat while I made phone calls and dealt with paperwork.

My challenges as a new mother and working outside the home continued to tax me. Trying to find a balance, a workable solution to the demands of career and motherhood, was a daily battle. It gave me empathy for and new understanding of other women conflicted between their callings and their roles as mothers. Was there an answer? I tried to find it as I tried to manage a national organization, albeit a small one, do volunteer work with the Evangelical Fellowship of Canada, and raise a toddler at the same time. I felt torn between my wonderful child and what I felt was important work for God. Whatever I was doing, I felt distracted by what I was *not* doing. Once again, I was fortunate to have friends and family, most importantly my husband, who supported me, prayed for me and helped with childcare.

When I was pregnant with my second child in 1994, it became clear that my lifestyle was not sustainable. I had realized even earlier that the CLF needed more than I could give it, as did my growing family. So, I gave my notice, trusting that God would lead me through this season. I felt a great sense of peace. The day I shipped the CLF files to the next leader, I went into labour. I was able to spend the next months focusing on being a mother to my young children. It truly was where I needed to be at that time.

## FORGIVENESS AND HUMILITY BUILD THE INNER STRENGTH EVERY LEADER NEEDS

Forgiveness is one of the great gifts of the Christian life, as it allows us to move on from being hurt and disappointed. The development journey for every leader brings unfulfilled dreams, unexpected setbacks and life detours. Pain and disappointment are written into life.

My most challenging experience of forgiveness was at the completion of my doctoral studies. My thesis supervisor had asked me to find a Canadian law professor to be one of my examiners. I chose a professor who taught with my husband and whom I considered to be a friend. It was devastating when she trashed my dissertation and recommended that I completely rewrite it. While I was humbled, God gave me the strength to make the changes needed to meet her concerns, and I passed and earned my doctorate.

After the doctoral thesis experience, I approached life with much more humility. I experienced a change of heart that gave me inner peace and much more compassion toward myself and others. I learned a valuable life lesson: "At the entry of every challenge or problem, we have to choose our attitude."

Often leaders think that their development journey will be like a straight line—no curves, setbacks or unexpected detours. Life does not give us that kind of fairy-tale story. The Bible is clear: "Don't blame fate when things go wrong—trouble doesn't come from nowhere. It's human! Mortals are born and bred for trouble as certainly as sparks fly upward" (Job 5:6–7, MSG).

The biblical writer James gives this perceptive on life's unexpected turns: "Count it all joy, my brothers, when you meet trials of various kinds, for you know that the testing of your faith produces steadfastness. And let steadfastness have its full effect, that you may be perfect and complete, lacking in nothing" (James 1:2–4).

Forgiveness builds character and inner strength. I had to learn about forgiveness yet another time. When we returned to Canada from South Africa, after my graduation from the University of Stellenbosch, in January 1, 1999, we thought we had the world by the tail. Don had applied for a tenure track position at the University of Saskatchewan law school. I had as well. We even proposed to job share. But I didn't even get an interview, despite having taught constitutional law there. Another professor was hired instead of Don. It became clear that God was closing doors in Saskatoon.

Once again we had to deal with our disappointment and pain and submit it to God. I would love to say that God teaches us about humility and forgiveness once or twice in a lifetime. It would be wonderful if one humbling experience alone could develop a permanently humble character. However, I find that learning humility and forgiveness is a continuous process. God brings us one challenge after another to develop our character in more profound ways and on deeper levels. I was slowly coming to understand a new reality in Romans 8:28: "And we know that for those who love God all things work together for good, for those who are called according to his purpose." I had to learn to trust rather than continuing to fight disappointment every time a plan went awry.

Another challenge to my humility came with my long-awaited opportunity to write a book. After years of studying religious freedom,

I gathered all my research and poured many hours and great effort into writing the manuscript. I felt confident about the outcome.

After I submitted my first draft, though, the publisher responded that I needed to rewrite the *entire* book "with more focus." What a humbling experience. I felt downright rejected. I had poured my knowledge, my soul and my experience into hours of writing, only to be met with a request to begin the process all over again.

If the book was to be published, I needed to swallow my pride and refocus. I learned that forgiveness, humility and letting go are deep spiritual experiences that open us up for God to work new miracles, His surprises. God blessed the outcome. *Fighting over God: A Legal and Political History of Religious Freedom in Canada* was published in 2014 by McGill-Queens University Press. I continue to work on international religious freedom and am an academic advisor to the International Institute for Religious Freedom. I have the privilege of speaking at conferences all over the world, to both academic and professional audiences.

New opportunities only became possible because I had worked through forgiveness and humility several times. Forgiveness. It's a gift, given by God's grace to expand and develop us. Forgiveness does not change the past, but it does enlarge our future.

## NEVER UNDERESTIMATE THE IMPACT OF "UNUSUAL" RELATIONSHIPS

Leadership is not just about working well with those who are like us and share our values and faith—it's about learning to find common ground with those very different from us, even those with whom we may profoundly disagree. My first experience of this came with a *Toronto Star* reporter.

It was May 2002, a very difficult month. My father had passed away. I was grieving, stressed and emotionally drained. A day after Dad's burial, still in my personal pain, I was back at work to attend a hearing on my complaint to the Ontario Press Council against the *Toronto Star* for a very anti-evangelical-Christian commentary. As I walked into the hearing, a woman introduced herself and asked me how I was doing. She no doubt intended it as a pleasantry. I responded that it was my first day back after burying my father and I was really quite shattered. She was sympathetic, even though she turned out to be the reporter from the *Toronto Star* who was arguing against me.

This was a defining moment for me. Would I succumb to intimidation? Would I allow my personal pain to override what I needed to do? Thankfully, I faced my opponent and was successful in my complaint. The *Toronto Star* was ordered to print an apology. The reporter was at the time, and still is, in the Ottawa bureau of the *Toronto Star*. Throughout the same-sex marriage debates and related media coverage our paths crossed again, yet she was always respectful of me, even though she clearly disagreed with my position. Being real with her forged an unusual relationship between us.

I soon had another experience where being willing to develop a relationship allowed great leadership impact. I returned to the EFC office in August 2003, after a year away in France, with bigger challenges facing me. The same-sex marriage issue in Canada had progressed but was by no means over. Those who sought to maintain the historic definition of marriage were losing court battle after court battle. My particular focus was on retaining religious freedom for clergy and religious institutions. As the EFC made a submission on this to the parliamentary committee holding hearings on the Civil Marriage Act in 2005, one of Don's former students, now a Bloc Quebecois MP, approached me about amendments to the bill that would protect religious institutions. The Bloc Quebecois was very supportive of changing the definition of marriage to include same-sex couples. It therefore surprised me that this MP would be willing not only to vote for an amendment but to introduce it and support it. And because it was a Bloc Quebecois MP who introduced the amendment, he was able to gain support where an MP from another political party might not have been able to get the amendment passed. While several others were also involved in negotiating, this personal relationship was the foundation for the amendments.

The years addressing the issue of the definition of marriage were the most difficult of my life. They were challenging spiritually and emotionally. Throughout, I had a small community of faithful friends who regularly prayed for me. In addition, there were many in the broader Christian community who prayed. I felt buoyed up at times and knew that prayers were being offered. Occasionally I met people, often women, who told me that they prayed for me daily by name and in their weekly Bible studies. I was moved to tears by this, as it was such a difficult time. God sometimes calls us to do difficult things. He always walks with us during these times, but it is crucial to draw on the deep well of resources in the Christian community as well.

## BE READY TO ACCEPT GOD-SIZED ASSIGNMENTS

My most stretching and challenging leadership assignment came when I accepted a position as professor at Trinity Western University and director of the Laurentian Leadership Centre in Ottawa. I didn't know at the time that I would be faced with another controversial issue and a much greater God-sized assignment than I could have imagined. It would require more faith and trust in the God who called me than ever before. Like Joshua, I needed courage. Yet I knew that if I obeyed and took the steps, God would equip me to be strong.

I have learned that in our leadership development, God will always give us roles and assignments that are far beyond us. We will require more faith, more trust and a greater dependency on God. This was my case at Trinity Western University. Robert Browning's poem "Andrea del Sarto" states, "A man's reach should exceed his grasp,/ Or what's a heaven for?"

Teaching, mentoring and learning from students at Trinity Western University has been a delightful experience for me. In my role at the Laurentian Leadership Centre, it's my responsibility to invest in upper-year students who are taking courses and completing a part-time internship. These are mostly millennials who are in transition from being students to engaging in the working world. Because we are located in Ottawa, we can observe the public policy process first-hand. I have regular interaction with Canada's political leaders, which adds to the classroom discussions on public policy and cultural change. Many of my students are in their own process of discovering their gifts and passions, and it's a privilege to see them find themselves and move to fulfill their callings. Investing my knowledge and experience into them as they start their own leadership development journeys is a privilege.

However, the more I became involved at Trinity, the more I felt ready for yet another challenge. And the opportunity came. In mid-2007, Trinity Western's president asked Kevin Sawatsky, dean of the School of Business, and me to start developing a proposal for a law school. This had been a dream of mine since 1993 and had been in the university's long-range plan for as long. It was a huge task, but we had help from lawyers, law professors and judges. We submitted our proposal in 2012, with a vision of equipping future lawyers to be professionals of competence and compassion, serving where there are unmet needs in society.

When I was at law school 30 years ago, I found it a very secular environment. It has only gotten more so. My vision is to see a law school at Trinity Western that will have a high level of excellence and competence and also will be a place where issues of integrating faith and practice are welcomed in the classroom. I would love to see law graduates practice law with faith and compassion throughout Canada.

In the summer of 2014, Trinity Western was looking to hire the first dean of law. It was widely expected that I would take on this position. I had a great deal of internal conflict over this, however. As before, I spent some time at the family cottage seeking to hear from God. His response was unmistakable; this was not a role that I was to take on at that time. Even I was surprised at what I sensed was being made clear to me by God. With a heavy heart, I did not apply. Within several months, the British Columbia minister of advanced education revoked our approval to proceed, putting the whole project on hold. I believe God held me back for this reason.

We didn't anticipate that the law school proposal would have significant backlash from the legal profession and legal academics, who deeply oppose Trinity Western's code of conduct, particularly the requirement that faculty and student abstain from sexual intimacy outside of opposite-sex marriage. Three law societies voted against graduates from our law school being able to practice law in their provinces. Trinity Western had taken a similar case to the Supreme Court of Canada with respect to beginning a college of education and succeeded in 2001. We thought that lawyers would respect a clear Supreme Court precedent. As well, the amended sections of the Civil Marriage Act that I worked on back in 2005 make it clear that there is room for diversity of beliefs about marriage. Again, Trinity Western has gone to the courts to stand for religious freedom. At this point, the Nova Scotia Court of Appeal ruled in favour of Trinity Western and the Ontario Court of Appeal ruled against. The British Columbia Court of Appeal ruled strongly in favor of Trinity Western. The Ontario and British Columbia cases have been appealed and are expected to be heard at the Supreme Court of Canada in 2017.

At times I have felt very discouraged that I am again embroiled in controversy over same-sex marriage and religious freedom. I thought

God had released me from that in 2006. But Kevin Sawatsky and Trinity Western's president, Bob Kuhn, were also engaged in previous court cases involving religious freedom. Rather than being discouraged that we seem to be in the same place again, I have come to see that God has equipped us to stand strong in the face of opposition.

*"Have I not commanded you? Be strong and courageous. Do not be afraid, do not be discouraged, for the* LORD, *your God will be with you wherever you go." (Joshua 1:9)*

Today, I understand God's Word to Joshua. My faith, my family and my community have kept me strong. In the words of Alfred, Lord Tennyson in his poem "Ulysses,"

> I am a part of all that I have met;
> Yet all experience is an arch wherethro'
> Gleams that untravell'd world whose margin fades
> For ever and forever when I move.

God has used my natural leadership abilities and my character to further His kingdom. He has given me the tools and the community to be able to fulfill His calling on my life. It takes courage to seize opportunities and stand strong in the face of opposition, but God sustains us through it all.

When I look back on my life, it is clear that God has led me from one thing to another; nothing was ever wasted with God. He used every experience to prepare me for what would come next. God has brought me to places and allowed me to work with people that are beyond what I ever dreamed possible. I have a wonderful and supportive family, meaningful work, and a deep and personal relationship with the Creator of the universe. I overflow with joy!

Janet Epp Buckingham is a professor at Trinity Western University (TWU) and the director of the prestigious Laurentian Leadership Centre, an Ottawa live-in extension program focusing on leadership in public policy, business and communications. Prior to her career at TWU, Janet served as executive director of the national Christian Legal Fellowship and also as legal counsel for the Evangelical Fellowship of Canada.

Janet researches and publishes on the topic of religious freedom with a focus on the intersection of faith, public policy and the legal system. She is a media commentator and public speaker on the Charter of Rights and human rights. Her recent book, *Fighting over God*, is a legal and political history of religious freedom in Canada. Janet has a key role in developing the proposal for the TWU School of Law in British Columbia. The mother of two adult children, she resides in Ottawa with her husband, Don.

# Journeying

## from Mother to Changemaker

by Joy Smith

L ife doesn't always turn out the way we think it will. But if we listen to and obey God's leading, God's plans for our lives will be fulfilled. We will see how God uses our influences and experiences to mould us into the leaders that will—perhaps to our surprise!—make a real difference in the world.

### A LESSON IN HUMILITY

My childhood was full of hardship but never lacking in love. My father was an immigrant from Iceland, a veteran of World War II and a proud Canadian. He never allowed his children to forget how privileged they were to live in Canada—a country with freedom of speech, freedom to worship and freedom to voice our concerns to the ruling government in Canada.

My siblings and I were careful not to take these freedoms for granted, but secretly I did not feel "privileged." Our family was poor. Despite the harsh Manitoba winters, my four siblings and I never had proper mitts, scarves or coats. The cold winters—sometimes reaching -40°C—caused frostbitten fingers and toes as we walked to and from school.

One day, Mom told me and my older sister Mae to go to a clothing store in Killarney and ask the owner if we could get some mitts, boots and scarves and put it on our parents' charge bill, which would be paid when the next baby bonus cheque arrived. I will never forget that day. We walked into the store, fully expecting to be able to buy the much-needed winter attire, but we were refused. The proprietor told us that our parents had not paid their last bill and he could not charge any more items. We hastily left the store, red-faced, and made our way back to school. I could hardly believe that man had sent us back out into the cold, knowing we had no mitts, scarves or winter boots. That incident made me understand that we were poor and on our own. But it also awakened me to the harsh reality of injustice in the world—a painful realization that God would use to fuel my later work.

At a young age, I began to understand why we had to hoe the garden, can and freeze the vegetables, and pluck and freeze the chickens. My attitude toward all the summer chores changed, and from then on I hoed the garden willingly under the hot sun. I wanted to help my parents and my siblings so they would be all right.

My siblings and I were often teased because we were so poor. We were teased about our clothes and teased about what was not in our lunches. (I envied the children with store-bought white bread and delicious cake and cookies!) There were bullies in our school, and their taunting was merciless! I was really scared when I saw my brother being beaten up in the schoolyard one recess. I was afraid to intervene. Instead, I ran into the schoolhouse to get the teacher to stop the fight. By the time she arrived on the scene, my brother was bloodied and bruised. I promised myself that I would never again run away when someone else was suffering before my eyes.

Looking back, I know that my family's faith in God is what helped us to survive. We always attended church—two services on Sunday, choir practice on Wednesday and youth group on Friday. Even though I heard the gospel many times as a child, I never actually accepted Christ into my heart until I was 19. That step of faith opened my heart to receive the gift of the Holy Spirit to guide me throughout my life. Little did I know how my relationship with God would grow and stretch from that point forward as God's plan for my life unfolded.

## A LESSON IN FORGIVENESS

I didn't always listen to the Holy Spirit's voice. There were many times when I had to stop and examine what I was doing and where I should be. Life was not always easy. I married young and divorced when my four children were still school-aged. I had a hard time forgiving myself and working through the challenges of being a single mom, but in hindsight, those tough years of fighting for my family were some of the happiest of my life.

My children were everything to me. I loved making their lunches before they went to school and listening to their stories. I worked as a teacher, which coincided well with the rhythms of a young family. My first leadership lessons were embedded in the daily challenges that I faced every day as a single working mom. Rising early in the morning, organizing my children, doing the household chores and helping with the never-ending homework instilled in me a sense of discipline and perseverance, which I would later draw on as a leader.

As a single mom, I often wondered how I could keep up my challenging teaching job and provide adequately for the needs of my children. Many times I allowed fear and doubt to creep into my heart. But through prayer I learned to let those fears go and carry on. I was often drawn to Psalm 23:1: "The LORD is my shepherd; I shall not want." I hung on to that promise. It sustained me.

Today many mothers underestimate the powerful roles they play in shaping the lives of their children, regardless of the circumstances they deal with from day to day. In spite of the long hours of work and the day-to-day challenges of raising my family, I always knew I was not alone. I always knew that God was with me. The passage from 1 Peter 5 was precious to me: "Humble yourselves, therefore, under God's mighty hand, that he may lift you up in due time. Cast all your anxiety on him because he cares for you" (1 Peter 5:6, NIV). What a much-needed reminder that I always had someone on my side!

Seven years after my divorce, I remarried—something I vowed I would never do again. However, God gave me the strength to forgive not only myself but others as well. I look back on this time period and understand why I needed to forgive. To have made my pain a shrine would have imprisoned me and blocked the calling on my life that was yet awaiting me. Forgiveness set me free to move ahead. I also learned that divorce does not stop God from working His will in our lives. We rise from the pain. We move forward.

By this time I had achieved a master's degree and was well into the teaching profession. I loved the smell of books in the library, the challenge of reaching into my students' minds and the excitement of knowing that when my students left my classroom, they could reach for the stars! I loved teaching. I wanted to be the principal of a school someday. I dreamed of making it the best high-academic-standard school in Canada. But God had other plans. Leadership always has an element of uncertainty even though we make our plans. God is mighty and God is near, working over and above what we desire for our lives and pulling us, like a magnet, to align with His plan.

## A LESSON IN PAIN AND EMPATHY

My eldest son, Edward, grew up to be a police officer. I was proud of his choice to use his courage and compassion to serve the community. As a new officer, Edward kept our family spellbound with his interesting stories of fighting crime. But as time went on, those stories stopped, and Edward began to withdraw emotionally.

My daughter Janet was the first to express concern. Janet shared how Edward would sometimes show up at her house late at night in full uniform and ask to hold her colicky baby, Matthew, all night. Edward never seemed to sleep. Early in the morning when Janet woke up, he would be gone.

We noticed that Edward's hair had turned grey almost overnight. I will never forget the day when I took my son aside and asked him how he was doing and what on earth was going on. I saw hurt in my son's eyes as he related some of the things he saw and experienced as a police officer in the child abuse unit and later in the Integrated Child Exploitation (ICE) unit. He told me about the images that he had to view of child abuse and sexual exploitation of the very young. It was excruciating to him. After viewing the images, his unit had to go find the abused children and rescue them from the predators.

When Edward left the ICE unit, his desk was stacked with files. Those files contained the names and faces of children who were yet to be rescued. Leaving those files with the faces of missing children filled Edward with overwhelming guilt. The effects of what he saw and experienced would haunt him for many years to come.

Edward's experience influenced me. As a concerned mother and a teacher, I began to educate the public on how to protect our youth from child predators online. I wanted children to be safe. Technology was advancing with no checks and balances, and children were being lured over the Internet. It was alarming to me. My passion for teaching about the dangers of human trafficking gradually led me to the streets to talk to the girls who were selling their bodies at night. I was shocked at their young age! As I listened to their stories, I distributed sandwiches and clothing and encouraged the girls to get off the streets.

It was true. Kids were being bought and sold—in Canada! The predators were picking the young because they were easy to lure, manipulate and intimidate. Furthermore, the business was lucrative—predators could make between $260,000 and $280,000 per victim per year.

The painful stories that I heard from Edward and from the young victims caught in this modern-day slavery prompted me to leave my chosen profession of teaching and fight for the victims of human trafficking. It was time to use the privilege that my father talked about so passionately—the privilege of voicing my concerns to the government. I turned to politics to make laws that would get these predators off the streets.

My son's pain became my pain. Pain is often the seedbed of setting our lives on a new course, a calling we were not aware of. Our pain is used as a catalyst to help others in pain. Can God use our pain to develop our character and leadership ability? Absolutely. God was developing in me a deep empathy and compassion for those suffering. The empathy I felt for the young victims would be a powerful motivating force when I faced future challenges and disappointments.

## A LESSON IN PATIENCE

After becoming a member of Parliament in 2004, I was determined to put an end to the human trafficking of women and children in our country. But it wasn't easy.

At first I thought that becoming a cabinet minister would allow me to influence Parliament to focus on the human trafficking issue in Canada. I was naive. I thought all parliamentarians knew about human trafficking and would work together to stop this crime. I quickly found out that almost no parliamentarian knew anything about human trafficking, and no one even believed it was happening in Canada! I was actually laughed at when I tried to bring the topic to the Status of Women Committee.

Sometimes my presentations fell on deaf ears. I learned what it meant to be "whipped"—a term meaning that those high in authority are trying to bring parliamentarians into line. "I can do all things through Christ" (Philippians 4:13, WEB) kept running through my mind as I continued to educate parliamentarians and advocate on behalf of the survivors of human trafficking. Attitudes gradually changed as parliamentarians learned more about the unsettling reality of human trafficking in Canada.

Throughout this experience, God was teaching me how to lead with patience and understanding. Without that patience, my leadership in this area would not have produced the results that were needed. Like Daniel in Old Testament times, I purposed in my heart to stay focused and remain strong. Spiritual maturity comes when we persevere. We ultimately win. And I did.

My motion to study human trafficking in Canada was passed by the Status of Women Committee on September 26, 2006, and the study began on October 3, 2006. This was my chance! I rallied witnesses who knew about human trafficking, and they testified. Those who used to laugh at me had tears in their eyes as they heard the stories of profound abuse and deception.

## A LESSON IN PERSEVERANCE

The study on human trafficking produced one of the most informative reports about sex trafficking authored in Canada. The Standing Committee on the Status of Women's February 2007 report, *Turning Outrage into Action to Address Trafficking for the Purpose of Sexual Exploitation in Canada*, was tabled in Parliament on February 27, 2007. The key priorities of the report focused on the prevention of trafficking, the protection of victims and the prosecution of offenders. This report prompted all parliamentarians and all Canadians to stand up for victims who are trafficked for the purpose of sexual exploitation, to support the proposed recommendations and to take whatever steps necessary to implement them.

In March 2007, motion M-153, which I introduced to the House of Commons in 2006, was unanimously passed. It stated, "The trafficking of women and children across international borders for the purposes of sexual exploitation should be condemned, and that the House call on the government to immediately adopt a comprehensive strategy to combat the trafficking of persons worldwide."

The perseverance that I had learned through raising my family and working with survivors of human trafficking helped me to stay focused on creating a precise plan with goals and timelines. Perseverance also helped me learn how to collaborate with many individual parliamentarians.

God knew that the workload was huge, and He brought to my office my chief of staff, Joel Oosterman, and his wife, Kristy. They proved to be invaluable, and their Christian walk and prayers did much to see me through and support me on my journey of faith.

## A LESSON IN COURAGE AND OBEDIENCE

The passing of motion M-153 led to my work on my first private member's bill, Bill C-268, An Act to Amend the Criminal Code (minimum sentence for offences involving trafficking of persons under the age of 18 years), which I introduced in 2009. At the time, Canada's Criminal Code provided a mandatory minimum sentence of five years for the aggravated offence of living off the avails of prostitution of a person under the age of 18 years. The trafficking of children is similar to this offence but often has much more severe consequences for the victim. Bill C-268 contained amendments to Canada's Criminal Code to provide a five-year minimum sentence for the trafficking of minors in Canada and a six-year minimum sentence for cases involving aggravated offences like assault or death.

During the time when I was working on Bill C-268, my husband was diagnosed with a serious cancer, an aggressive large B-cell lymphoma. He went through four years of chemo, then a stem cell transplant, and finally, in the fifth year, when nothing worked, his body was invaded with rigorous radiation treatments. The prognosis wasn't good. It was very difficult for me to stay the course and steer Bill C-268 through the parliamentary process. It was an unpopular bill initially because it was a private member's bill and few knew that human trafficking was prevalent in Canada. There were times when I wanted to quit. A particularly difficult time was when my youngest sister passed away and my husband's cancer treatments increased.

I kept praying. I marvelled every evening when my husband left the house, leaning on a homemade walking stick to support his frail body, walking to the end of the driveway. I could see him raise his face to the stars, and I knew he was praying. This activity took place almost every night. What I had worked hard for was about to happen, but it came in one of the darkest times in my life.

The day came for my husband's transplant. Regrettably, he became very ill, shaking profusely. He asked me to buy some type of juice he thought he could keep down. I hurried to Safeway. It was pouring rain, and I was alone in my car. It was the loneliest feeling. As I pulled up into the parking lot, my phone rang. Joel Oosterman excitedly told me that the bill I had worked so hard for was receiving royal assent and was soon to be embedded in the law! I will never forget that day. The rain was pouring down, and I was alone in the car. I could hear everyone shouting in the background. What a joyful noise! Suddenly I didn't feel alone anymore. I just closed my eyes and said, "Thank You, God."

When Bill C-268 passed, it successfully amended section 279.01 of Canada's Criminal Code to create a new offence for child trafficking with a five-year mandatory penalty. This was only the 15th time in Canadian history that a private member's bill amended the Criminal Code. I knew that this was God's work, not mine. I was the tool He used because I was willing. And when I felt discouraged or overwhelmed, God gave me the strength to keep going.

## A LESSON IN ENGAGING SOCIETY

Despite the success of Bill C-268, I came to realize that ending human trafficking cannot be done with legislation alone; it is a task that must be embraced by society as whole. We must continue to educate and encourage Canadians to speak up, to consider their words and actions and to engage others. So in 2010 I launched a proposal titled "Connecting the Dots." This piece provided key recommendations to be part of a national action plan. The recommendations included providing adequate funding for NGOs to deliver care, counselling, shelter and assistance to victims; developing policies and regulations to combat forced labour and child labour abroad; and creating regional human trafficking taskforces.

Following the release of "Connecting the Dots," the federal government began drafting Canada's first National Action Plan to Combat Human Trafficking. It would be a comprehensive blueprint to guide the fight against the serious crime of human trafficking in our nation. On June 6, 2012, the action plan was launched. The new measures emphasized in the plan, totalling over $25 million over four years, built and strengthened Canada's significant work to date to prevent, detect and prosecute human trafficking.

God placed on my heart the need for a national action plan to create programs and assistance for survivors of human trafficking. At the same time, the need to address human trafficking issues abroad weighed heavily on my heart. It became clear to me that a law needed to be put in place to bring to justice Canadians and permanent residents of Canada who prey on innocent victims in countries abroad. My next bill and the national action plan were more steps of obedience.

The national action plan, which provided programs and rehabilitation services for victims of human trafficking, was launched on June 6, 2012. This national action plan had components that supported Bill C-268, so survivors of human trafficking would have the support systems they needed so badly. In addition, there was a framework where police and others could work together to suppress this heinous crime in our country.

There was overwhelming support for Bill C-310 from law enforcement, victims' services, Indigenous peoples' representatives and religious and secular non-governmental organizations. Overall, Bill C-310 allowed the long arm of the Canadian law into other countries by allowing Canadian police to go abroad and bring to Canada for trial any Canadian citizen or a permanent resident of Canada suspected of trafficking people abroad. Bill C-310 received royal assent and became law on June 28, 2012.

That was a memorable month!

On February 13, 2014, I released "The Tipping Point," a report developed in response to the Supreme Court of Canada's ruling in *Canada v. Bedford* that the Canadian prostitution laws were unconstitutional. The ruling left our country at a tipping point, and we had to ensure that our nation's response decisively protected women and communities for generations to come.

I prepared "The Tipping Point" to provide Canadians with an idea of how the Nordic model of prostitution functions and successfully provides the tools to prevent sex trafficking and exploitation of women and youth. Countries such as Norway and Sweden have made substantive progress toward eliminating human trafficking by targeting the market, eliminating the demand, supporting victims and placing the ownership for these crimes on the perpetrators. The report also made recommendations on how Canada could adopt its own version of the Nordic model.

June 4, 2014, was a historic day for Canada! Justice minister Peter MacKay introduced Bill C-36, The Protection of Communities and Exploited Persons Act, in response to the Supreme Court of Canada's decision in *Canada v. Bedford*. Under Bill C-36, for the first time in Canada's history, the buying of sexual services would be illegal, prostituted/trafficked women would not be treated as a nuisance but treated with dignity, and the government of Canada would provide robust funding to help women and youth escape prostitution. Johns arrested for purchasing or attempting to purchase sex would face stiff fines and/or jail time. Bill C-36 also strengthened offences targeting pimps and traffickers and criminalized the advertising of the sexual services of others. We had turned a corner in the fight to end human trafficking and prostitution.

"The Tipping Point" influenced the outcomes of Bill C-36. Traditionally, women were arrested far more often than men for what was called "prostitution." "The Tipping Point" provided new information and shone a light on human trafficking and how the predators work to gain the trust of their victims. In time, these young people were forced into the sex trade, and their lives would be changed forever. "The Tipping Point" led the way so these young women would not be arrested but be given a chance to rebuild their lives through rehabilitation, education and a chance to restart their lives. Bill C-36 provided these recommendations under the Canadian law.

Over the next ten months I worked closely with the government, NGOs, survivors and law enforcement in the development and adoption of Bill C-36. On December 6, 2014, Canada's National Day of Remembrance and Action on Violence Against Women, Bill C-36 came into force.

## FINAL WORDS TO LEADERS

My journey has taught me that whenever I come face to face with an opportunity to obey God's calling, there is always pushback. My faith in God and His grace is the one thing that is always with me in times of defeat and in times of triumph. I have come to know that we can do all things through Christ who strengthens us, as God's Word tells us in Philippians 4:13.

I've also come to understand that we wrestle not against flesh and blood but against principalities and powers and things unseen (Ephesians 6:12). I am constantly reminded that the gift of the Holy Spirit is always with us after we receive Christ as our personal Saviour.

I've left politics to work full time with the Joy Smith Foundation "to ensure that every Canadian man, woman, and child is safe from manipulation, force, or abuse of power designed to lure and exploit them into the sex trade or forced labour." We must continue to fight to end this brutal crime. The bills are in place to bring the perpetrators to justice. Now we have to use education to ensure we put an end to human trafficking in Canada.

Here is a summary of my top leadership advice:

- Embrace what you gain from your early beginnings in character and life-building values, because these will shape your calling and who you will become.
- What may seem like failure can be used by God to channel you into new possibilities.
- Pain is often the catalyst to your future. You can curse it or embrace it.
- Perseverance is a discipline not achieved in one day or even a year.
- To fulfill God's plan for his or her life, a leader will move from independence to dependence. You cannot complete God's tasks without total dependence on Him.
- Prayer is your lifeline to inner strength, wisdom, discernment and direction. Learn to pray.

Life doesn't always turn out the way we think it will. But it will turn out the way God planned. All we have to do is listen to His almighty voice. Being elected to the Parliament of Canada is not something I dreamed about as a young child growing up in rural post-war Manitoba. And yet, that is where God led me. Looking back, I can see how God patiently shaped my character for the work that He had prepared in advance for me to do (see Ephesians 2:10). Every lesson was a building block—though the painful lessons, at the time, seemed more like roadblocks. My story is a story of God's faithfulness and His relentless pursuit of justice and freedom for the oppressed.

After a 23-year teaching career in Manitoba, Joy Smith became a member of Parliament. Since her election in 2004, she has worked with leaders at the federal and international levels to advance legislation and initiatives to combat modern-day slavery and to provide assistance to survivors. Joy is recognized as a leading Canadian anti-human-trafficking advocate and has received numerous awards, including the United Nations Women Canada Recognition of Achievement Award and the Wilberforce Award.

Joy was instrumental in passing two bills that made Canadian history: Bill C-268 enforces tough child trafficking penalties, and Bill C-310 allows law enforcement to arrest Canadians if they engage in human trafficking abroad. Joy also worked with the minister of justice in the development and passage of Bill C-36, ground-breaking legislation that changed Canada's approach to prostitution. Today she devotes her time to the Joy Smith Foundation.

# *Translating*

## Vision into Reality

by Margaret Gibb

I couldn't believe what I was hearing!

"Would Margaret Kerychuk come and read Job chapter 1 for us?" Hearing my name requested as a Scripture reader in church made my whole body freeze. My energy level plummeted to an all-time low.

My mind whirled. *What? Why didn't the pastor at least ask my permission? Doesn't he know that I can't do this? I'm not a public speaker. I'm not a public anything!*

To read in front of the congregation and my future husband was terrifying. Bob had won several awards for public speaking and was the student minister of this congregation. As we faced marriage and pastoral ministry together, I felt very secure in his platform ability, but facing the reality of my limitations in this public setting was awkward and humiliating. *This could be the end of our engagement*, I thought as I tried to think of my next step.

Fear gripped me. *Where is Job? In the Old Testament or the New Testament?* I couldn't remember.

I flipped to the index page in my Bible. My finger slid down the list of Bible books. Job, page 465. I turned the pages quickly and made my wobbly legs move to the platform.

At the pulpit, I didn't look up at the people. With a dry mouth and trembling voice, I tried to read. Simple words became hard to pronounce. I stumbled badly through the first chapter.

When I finished, the pastor got up, cleared his throat and politely said, "Thank you."

Throughout the rest of the service, I didn't look up or look around me. I didn't even look at my future husband. The atmosphere in the car as we drove away from the church was silent and tense. I finally broke the awkwardness: "Bob, now you know. I will help you fulfill what you are called to do, but I cannot function on a platform. What happened today must never happen again." He took my hand and said, "It will be okay!"

It took many years for it to become okay!

## EARLY BEGINNINGS SHAPE LEADERSHIP DEVELOPMENT

My story begins 200 miles north of Edmonton—in a no-man's land. My grandparents arrived in Canada as part of a huge immigration from Ukraine in the late 1920s. They were looking for a better life in Canada but didn't realize that they would be asked to settle unbroken dense forestland. Bonnyville was the closest settled area.

The people in this wave of immigration were approved to come to Canada not because of their education or profession but because of their strong calloused hands. They built temporary shacks and barns for shelter and safety. They cleared rocks and trees, broke the land, planted vegetable gardens and braved bitter winter weather.

Life was primitive and hard, but difficulty has a way of bringing people together. My grandparents were part of a community bonded by a fierce resolve to succeed in the land they had dreamt about. There was no thought of returning to Ukraine; they had to survive and succeed in Canada.

Church was at the centre of their lives. My grandfather, Karp Hrycauk, had an outstanding influence as a pastor in the area. He started 25 churches by evangelizing in small communities in northern Alberta. His faith led him to walk for miles in -40°C winter temperatures to preach. Great care was taken when he arrived in a warm homestead kitchen to tend to his frozen feet. It was this kind of faith and commitment that he and my grandmother passed down to their nine children.

My mother, Nida, was Karp's eldest daughter. She was a slim, pretty girl who was also very smart. Grandfather Karp and my grandmother, Anna, had chosen a husband for my mother when she was only 16 years of age. His name was Paul, and he was a handsome, fun-loving, guitar-strumming young man. Anna was especially fond of Paul and told him outright to propose to her daughter.

Paul took the big step and proposed to my mom by letter. No dating—just a proposal—and my mom accepted.

Three months into marriage, Mom knew she was pregnant, but she suffered from intense headaches. The headaches only got worse as the pregnancy progressed. The only medication she had available was aspirin. To go into town, some 25 miles away, to see a doctor about a headache was deemed unnecessary. Mom took the aspirin but didn't know that her blood pressure was very high. Her self-prescribed medicating was not helping.

A few days before the birth of her child, Mom's headache reached the migraine level. Her legs were swollen, and her pulse was weak. She woke up in the middle of the night and stumbled out of bed to try to reach a pee bucket, but she fell beside a hot potbelly stove, burning her arm and leaving her unconscious on the floor. The loud thump awakened my father. He rushed to her side and yelled for help. My mother was having contractions and convulsions. They thought she was dying.

Dad ran to get help from a nearby neighbour. It took 7 hours before a makeshift ambulance—a truck with a chain-smoking driver—to arrive and take my mother to the hospital in Bonnyville, some 25 miles away.

My mother had eclampsia, a form of toxemia of pregnancy, characterized by convulsions.

When the doctor examined Mom, he said to my father, "I can save either your wife or your baby, but I cannot save both." The doctor took extreme care of my mom. He gave her seven pints of blood and worked hard to save her life.

Desperate, Dad called on God to save his wife and his baby. "I don't know if You will give us a boy or a girl, but this child has a destiny, a calling. Save my baby's life!" Several hours later, I was born.

*"Before I formed you in the womb I knew you, before you were born I set you apart; I appointed you."* (Jeremiah 1:4–5, NIV)

My miracle birth was the foundation of my calling, an appointment I did not understand until much later in life.

I grew up in a happy but disciplined home. For the first six years of my life, I lived on a farm. My playmates were sometimes my two brothers, Larry and Mike, but mostly the farm chickens! I spoke only Ukrainian until I was six, and I had Ukrainian names for the chickens I played with.

After the death of my grandfather, my dad, at only 27 years of age, assumed the responsibility of caring for his family, his mother and his two sisters. This change necessitated a move to the big city of Edmonton. What can an ex-farmer do in the big city of Edmonton? My dad had the stressful task of finding himself and his niche in life while providing for his family.

We moved into a large nine-room, three-storey house with one washroom and a small kitchen. My grandmother and her two daughters came to live with us; plus we took on boarders. My grandmother was the family cook, and Mother found work in a local dairy, packing butter into boxes. If farm life was survival, this was another kind of survival.

My two brothers and I did not have bedrooms of our own. We slept wherever we could. First one to find a bed got it!

Having as many as 10 boarders in our house made our home a place of constant activity with many interesting scenarios. I remember one Saturday before she left for work, Mom asked me to wash the kitchen floor and the stairs up to the third floor. I was happy to do so, even though I was only about eight years old. I was helping my mom! One boarder, as he stepped over my body to reach the top step, said, "Child labour." I hadn't heard that term before.

My elementary years were not fun. I felt very lost trying to fit into an English environment. I was very embarrassed to be Ukrainian and felt that the more popular children from English, Scottish and Irish backgrounds were more accepted by the teachers. It didn't help me either when I had to present that dreaded note from my father to excuse me from square dancing!

During the 1950s in Edmonton, Ukrainian people felt a measure of displacement. Multiculturalism was relatively new. The term "DP," or "displaced person," was commonly used. Polish and Ukrainian jokes were part of everyday vocabulary. Many people felt they were bypassed for promotions, awards or recognition because of their origin. As a result, ethnic groups kept to their own communities. Our family attended a Ukrainian church, and most of our friends were Ukrainians.

## GROWTH IN LEADERSHIP DEPENDS ON SURRENDER

When I was about 12 years of age, I surrendered my life to Jesus. My grandmother heard me all night call out His name, "Jesus!" This commitment sealed my determination to live my life for God.

My calling to live for Christ was affirmed at a special service with an evangelist in Edmonton. My mom took me to the service to be prayed for, since I had not been well. After I went forward for prayer ministry, the evangelist turned and addressed the congregation. "God is going to take this young girl," he said, "and use her in ministry to this nation and beyond." This statement had little meaning for me at the time.

I loved music and would often tinker at the church piano. My parents noticed my interest. With the extra income generated by the boarders, they decided to purchase a piano for me. Without lessons, I quickly figured out that a simple song only needs three chords. Playing the piano was my love and escape. I could sit for hours, just trying to find a new chord or sound. I basically taught myself to play the piano, which did me well after I became a pastor's wife and had many opportunities to play piano at church.

I found high school difficult, not so much for the studies but for the difficulty of fitting in. As a teenager my insecurity was real and deep. My plain looks, my moments of social awkwardness and my feelings of loneliness were constant struggles. I spent many lonely days wondering what life would bring me. I was afraid of people, afraid of the future and afraid of life. Worry was my middle name! I felt that I would never measure up and meet the expectations people had of me. I was in a self-inflicted prison and didn't know how to get out.

Conversations with my parents about my shyness would usually end in a stalemate. I couldn't articulate my true inner feelings. I didn't know it, but my parents were concerned about my future and my ability to handle life.

Many times I poured myself into Psalm 139, an amazing passage of Scripture on perception and healing: "For you created my inmost being;

you knit me together in my mother's womb. I praise you because I am fearfully and wonderfully made; your work are wonderful, I know that full well" (Psalm 139:13–14, NIV).

My prayer conversations with God were a mixture of fear and worry, as well as hope and worship. I was in an inner battle and knew it. But one thing I knew for certain: I loved God and desperately wanted to live out my life in service, whatever that meant. I didn't know it, but God was calling me to Himself. The process was just beginning and would continue for many years.

I would learn much later in life that inner struggle is important because it brings us to prayers of surrender and relinquishment, which open the heart to hope, healing worship and inner freedom.

During my high school years, my father, besides being an award-winning salesman for Sears Canada, was also the pastor of a small church in the east side of Edmonton. The small congregation was a mixture of older Ukrainian grandmas and couples with young children. My brothers and I were the only teenagers. We literally pastored with my father. We were the custodians, worship leaders and Sunday school teachers. We did whatever was needed to help him. We become problem solvers and visionaries with him. My father wanted our advice even as teenagers on church matters. We were part of his team! "What do you think?" was his common question to us.

We especially loved it when visiting pastors, missionaries or evangelists came to our church. The fun and fellowship in our home after a service when Mom laid out a lavish meal brought much joy to us and made rich connections and lasting memories.

Just as church had been at the centre of life for our dad in his younger years, so it became the centre of our lives as teenagers. I never had a time in my life when I didn't like church.

The calling of God on my life was a natural outflow of what I came to love in being a pastor's daughter. I knew ministry was for me! It was my fit. Yet I felt overwhelmed because of my deep insecurities. Attempting to step out into my calling only added to my fears. The only way my calling could be fulfilled, I thought, was through marriage.

One day I earnestly prayed my yes to God. "God," I prayed, "if You bring me a man who is called to be a pastor, I will fulfill my call through him. But never ask me to speak publicly, and never ask me to go to Africa!"

Our early beginnings shape and influence us but don't define us. God has established our sovereign foundations, those areas we have no control over: parents, extended family, when and where we were born and our circumstances. We are divinely positioned into families for a reason. My Ukrainian heritage and the values passed on to me proved, in time, to be an asset, not a liability.

At my high school graduation, a professor from the University of Alberta gave a three-point challenge that impacted me as I faced my future: Learn to live. Learn to love. Learn to learn. I lived out these words of wisdom by enrolling at Eastern Pentecostal Bible College (EPBC, now Master's College) in September 1962. I felt that I needed to leave Edmonton and force myself to come out of my inner bondage to discover my real self. I needed a new environment, a new place of belonging where I could begin again.

Leaving my family to begin my first year as a student at EPBC in Peterborough, Ontario, was a brave move, a daring move for me. At that time, enrolling in a college 2,000 miles from home was not common. I didn't know anyone at the college of 300 students except the academic dean, Dr. C. A. Ratz, a friend of my father's. But EPBC was the place God had purposed for my life.

The first four months were sheer hell. Terribly homesick, I hardly spoke to anyone. I went to class and then darted in and out of the dining room, only to go back to my room and write letters to my family at home. I hardly communicated with my roommate. I was lonely, afraid and scared.

After four months of grieving, I returned home for Christmas break. My excitement to be home was quickly replaced by lingering questions: Was this really home? Why didn't I feel like I belonged? I had a growing sense that Edmonton wasn't home anymore. Maybe my Ukrainian blood was kicking in and pushing me to grow up and not just survive but succeed in a new place in life.

When I returned to college, I decided to audition for the EPBC travelling ensemble that represented the school at many functions and churches. My alto voice got me in! Then I joined the yearbook team and worked with a group of literary students who loved writing and journalism. I signed up for Africa Prayer Band because it was the only mission field that tugged at me. (Praying for a continent, I thought, was very different from consenting to go!)

College life was rich with classes, guest speakers, spiritual emphasis days, student camaraderie and prayer times. It became home. I began to build friendships and discover the healing power of belonging. My two roommates, Ruth Edwards Croft and Margaret McLaughlin Sprackett, and I formed a strong friendship and soul sisterhood where we found in each other our "second self." We understood each other. Through countless conversations and college experiences, I began to break away from my shyness, insecurity and fear. I was released to believe in my own God-given potential and encouraged through friendship to believe in myself.

"The glory of friendship," wrote Ralph Waldo Emerson, "is the spiritual inspiration that comes to one when you discover that someone else believes in you and is willing to trust you with friendship." There is a divine positioning in life when God places people in our lives for our good and growth. These two friends, Margaret and Ruth, were divinely positioned for me.

I was coming alive and knew it! Confidence was springing up. I worried less and believed more. I finally felt I had something to offer. My future looked bright and not fearful.

In my third year, I was appointed as the social convener, a position that did not require public speaking, only organizational skills. I was finding my true self!

One cold winter night, a team of us singers and speakers was headed to a church outside of town for the weekend. Immediately we encountered black ice. Rather than returning to Peterborough and cancelling our assignment, we decided to drive slowly on the slippery highway. Coming toward us was a truck. As the driver approached us, his wheels spun on the black ice, and he hit our vehicle on the driver's side, causing the rear door to swing open. I was thrown from the car and rolled in a fetal position to the other side of the road. Our car kept spinning in circles, miraculously missing me.

When our car finally came to a stop, my team ran to me and found me with head lacerations but alive. The first car coming toward us stopped. Remarkably, it was the pastor of one of the Pentecostal churches in Peterborough, who recognized us as students from the college. He took me into his car and drove me to the hospital, where I received treatment. I was later sent back to the college. For a second time God spared my life.

Bob and I met in college. He was a known youth leader from Windsor, Ontario, with great speaking ability. On our first date, I tried my best to make conversation. I boldly said, "I don't know much about cars, but I know this is a Pontiac." (It wasn't!) My later fumbling through Job 1 didn't divert him from seeing my potential to be his helpmate in ministry. We were married on August 20, 1966, and were ready for ministry. At least we thought so. We assumed too quickly that because God called us, we were ready.

## LEADERS ARE STUDENTS OF LIFE

Roles for pastors' wives in the 1960s to 1980s were well-defined. Through both spoken and unspoken expectations, women like me knew how to fit into the role of being a pastor's wife. The fact that I could play the piano was always an advantage for Bob and me. Churches were more than happy to have a built-in pianist in the pastoral couple!

I was happy as a married woman and being in ministry with Bob. Deep down, I knew that pastoral ministry would change me. What I didn't know was that my secular work opportunities would equally change me.

Our first pastoral assignment was at Stone Church, Toronto, where Bob was asked to be youth pastor. Living in the downtown Toronto area was a dream. I found employment at IBM and loved the challenge of learning something new in an office environment.

The manager I worked with had great office organizational skills. Surprisingly to me, I understood what he was doing and trying to achieve. We were on the same page. The learning curve at IBM was energizing and stimulating. My knowledge was broadening, and my confidence continued to grow.

But after two wonderful years in Toronto, Bob was anxious to have his own church, and we were approached to pastor in South Porcupine, Ontario. Sadly, I had to resign from my job, much to the dismay of my manager, who felt I had a career with IBM.

I didn't like the north. I didn't understand the culture of the north, and I didn't like the terrain. I missed city life, my work, shopping malls and high-heeled shoes.

I shed many tears because of loneliness and feeling lost. Robert Clinton, in his remarkable book *The Making of a Leader*, calls the type of experience we had in the north an "isolation test," a time when a leader is separated from normal involvement or can be very involved yet in an isolated season.[15]

I was too young to appreciate the people of South Porcupine and enjoy this unique season in our lives. I didn't have a strong mentor in my life at that time. Some tests in leadership are difficult only because of our limited understanding of God's bigger picture. Mentoring is critical to help us gain perspective. I would learn later on in life that the best mentoring comes out of the place of pain in our own lives.

The great gift given to Bob and me at that time was the birth of our son. Tim was everything that Bob and I had dreamed of for our first child. He was God's gift to us in a season of isolation.

We accepted the very next invitation that came our way, which led us to Long Sault, a small village created when the St. Lawrence Seaway was built in 1959 and a delightful area of Eastern Canada on the Long Sault Parkway, near Upper Canada Village.

When we came to Long Sault, after only pastoring for one and a half years in South Porcupine, we were determined to stay a long time. The people were wonderful and received us well. But with a weekly attendance of about 40 people, our small congregation was only able to pay us a salary of $60 a week. We lived in a manse (parsonage), which helped our financial situation, but we struggled to make ends meet. I resisted the urge to find work outside the home, because my boy was seven months old and needed me.

One day while we were enjoying supper at the Long Sault Parkway, I noticed that the waste bins were filled with pop cans left by campers from the weekend before. With excitement I went to Bob and said, "Why don't we collect all the pop cans in all the bins within seven miles of the parkway and redeem them at the store? That will bring us some cash." Bob wasn't convinced, but we did try. We filled our car with pop cans several times but quickly realized that this would not solve our financial problem. I had to find work.

After much searching and one devastating rejection, I was invited to interview for a three-month position with Parks Canada at a pay rate of $100 a week. The interview was successful, and I got the job!

Working for Parks Canada was a definite God-answer, not just for the pay but also, primarily, for my leadership development. I was hired as

---

[15] J. Robert Clinton, *The Making of a Leader* (Colorado Springs: Navpress, 1988), 161.

administrative clerk for the interpretation department, working with 19 naturalists and interpreters in the national park system. I managed all the travel schedules for the staff, kept up the media resources library, wrote a manual, travelled to the various parks to work with their administrative support staff and worked with the regional director on five-year strategic planning. In developing the administrative section, I eventually had to hire two people to work with me. Parks Canada taught me that I had the ability to build. I instinctively knew what to do. It was a gift.

What started with pop cans ended up as an eight-year position with Parks Canada that prepared me for my future. The experience taught me that hidden opportunities for growth and development are never far away from what seems to be failure!

Working with Parks Canada, raising my son and being highly involved in our church—which grew to over 100 people—made my life very full. I was extremely busy and fulfilled, except for one thing—my prayer life.

I didn't have enough time in my day to set aside for personal devotions. I prayed in my car as I drove to work and on the run—"Bless me" and "Get me" kind of praying. During prayer times at church, I would write out my grocery list or compile a to-do list for work because my mind was somewhere else. I didn't know what to say to God after three minutes!

I remember one day driving home from work with much frustration at God's call to pray, yelling out, "Do You want to bring me to burnout? I don't have time to pray! I have no more minutes left in my day!" Yet God's Spirit was calling me.

There came a time when something moved in my heart. The desire to build a career with Parks Canada ended. Something deep was stirring me toward women's ministry. My mind would often go to a dreaming place of planning conferences for women and encouraging them. Like a seed in good soil, that dream desire grew stronger and stronger. I could not ignore it!

I could identify with Charles Swindoll, who wrote, "You know there has to be more, you're just not sure how to get there. One thing is certain, you just don't want to stay where you are at."[16]

One late afternoon, I left work in Cornwall and walked toward my car, which was parked a few blocks away. I stopped at a street corner,

---

[16] Charles Swindoll, quoted in Debbie Alsdorf, *Deeper, Living the Reality of God's Love* (Grand Rapids: Fleming H. Revell, 2008), 13.

looked up at the sky and heard a strong word from God: "I will give you a ministry to women. Follow Me." I was so exhilarated, I wanted to run! I knew that my time with Parks Canada was coming to an end. Something new was opening up.

A few weeks later Bob was called to a church in Montreal. It was 1978—not a good time for a unilingual English couple with a child in elementary school to move to the province of Quebec. Premier Lévesque, founder of the PQ party, was in power. Politically, Quebec was in turmoil. English-speaking people were closing their bank accounts and moving to Ontario. Large corporations were relocating to other parts of Canada. In spite of receiving many questions and even criticism, Bob and I knew that this church was for us.

If ever there was a "dream church," Greenfield Park was that for us! The church numbered some 250 people on a Sunday morning. There were many couples our age, the youth group was strong and the women's ministry was vibrant. The people loved Bob's preaching and his ability to make biblical stories come alive. We had good staff and capable church leaders.

We had been in Montreal less than a month and were still settling into our home when one Sunday night my back became incredibly sore. I felt weak and sick and didn't think I could play the piano that night for the evening service. I lay on a back pew throughout the service, wondering what was wrong. That night at home, I awakened Bob at 3:00 a.m. and asked him to take me to the closest hospital; something was desperately wrong.

A gynecologist was called in and ordered X-rays. I had an ectopic pregnancy (a "tubal pregnancy") and needed to have immediate surgery. I'd already had two miscarriages, and the thought of not being able to have another child was more than I could bear. The two miscarriages had happened in Long Sault and were difficult times as I grieved the losses. Now I was facing it again but with greater complications.

I was hospitalized for ten days. The doctor told me that the fallopian tube had been at the point of rupturing, which could have been fatal. For the third time, God spared my life.

Giving up the dream of having another child was very hard on Bob and me. We loved our son dearly, but my mother heart longed for a daughter!

A year and a half later, I was pregnant again. I felt very afraid. I experienced the same symptoms that I had during my miscarriages. My strong British-accented doctor knew my history and with a demanding voice said, "If you listen to me and get absolute bed rest for the next two weeks, you will save this baby!" I did, and Tricia Renee was born on August 13, 1981—a miracle baby. The girl we wanted!

It had been 11 years since I'd had a baby, and, frankly, I didn't know what to do! I was thrust back into the baby world of diapers, feedings and midnight pacing. I once again struggled to fit in and handle this new adjustment. A kind woman in our church offered to take care of Tricia once a week just to give me a needed break.

The nudge to pray that started back in Long Sault was still with me. So, rather than using my free day to shop or be with girlfriends, I decided to use the time to pray. This was one of the best decisions I made, for it turned my life in new directions.

## PRAYER ALWAYS RESULTS IN TRANSFORMATION

For the next two and a half years, I spent an hour and a half each day in prayer. I included the discipline of praying Scripture, starting with the letter to the Ephesians. The depth of Paul's prison prayers challenged me. His level of praying was from a place I did not understand, compared to my self-absorbed and often venting prayers. What I experienced in that two-and-a-half-year period was not a natural effort to pray but a call to prayer. I started prayer journaling at this time.

The deeper I moved into intercessory prayer, the more I saw. It was 1983. I was concerned about the separation issue in Quebec and the state of society and its impact on teenagers, like my son. I cut out a map of Canada and began praying for cities and provinces. The more I prayed, the more I realized that other women needed to join together to pray for our nation.

I began to pray in desperation, "Lord, call a woman to call women to prayer." I would suggest names to God of women who were smart and articulate and could address audiences of women. As time passed, I grew desperate, sincerely praying one day, "God, anyone will do; just call someone."

Within days, the phone rang. Would I be willing to speak to the women's group at Evangel Church? It would be a gathering of about 50 women. I explained graciously that I wasn't a public speaker and that I couldn't do what the woman was asking. Our district superintendent, Rev. Dick Bombay, was in our home that day and overheard my conversation. He interrupted me and said, "You don't close a door that God has just opened." I accepted the invitation and spoke on the only topic I knew about: prayer.

It has been said that big doors swing open from small hinges. This was the beginning of expansion for me! Immediately after this speaking event, I began receiving invitations to speak in other churches in Montreal. I was asked to be the women's ministry co-coordinator for Montreal, which required me to form a planning team. With a team in place, we began to dream of what we could do together in Montreal. We started with women's conferences, then quarterly city-wide prayer meetings, then added leadership training sessions for women.

Our church embraced the call to prayer. Bob preached it, practised it and encouraged it, and I started a women's prayer group. The youth especially responded. In a five-year period, 30 of our youth went to Bible college, 24 of whom are in ministry today in various parts of the world.

Soon I was introduced to Eileen Stewart Rhude, the national director of women's ministry, and she invited me to speak at her first national conference for women in Oakville, Ontario. She expected some 80 women, but over 200 registered. She asked me to speak on prayer.

This was beyond my reach, and I knew it! Minutes before I was scheduled to speak, I asked to be alone in the pastor's office. I lay on the floor and prayed to God, "Remember, I am the shy 16-year-old who vowed that I would never speak publicly. Please help me as I speak!"

The response to my message, "The Dynamics of Prayer," was more than I ever expected. I challenged the women to join a company of other women to pray, and I called for a public response. They responded, and I was overwhelmed!

After I gave the message, provincial leaders came to me with invitations to speak at their conferences and retreats. I was invited to Alberta, British Columbia, Newfoundland, the Maritimes and Saskatchewan. Canada opened up to me.

When I arrived home, Bob Skinner, the editor of *The Pentecostal Testimony*, called me and asked for permission to publish my message

in the next issue, January 1986. That was the first of several messages I shared at national women's ministry conferences that were featured in *The Pentecostal Testimony*, which launched my writing career.

Eileen and I started establishing a national prayer network, linking approximately 1,000 churches and 6,000 intercessors. Later, I was one of the few women speakers to be on the speakers' roster for the Congress on Pentecostal Leadership in Toronto. For eight years I travelled Canada, fulfilling in part the prophetic word given over me when I was a child.

After 12 years of rewarding ministry in Greenfield Park, Bob and I once again felt a stirring and knew that our work was done. We accepted a call to pastor Bethel Church in Brandon, Manitoba. From the outset we knew that our adjustment to life in Manitoba and its culture would have some challenges, but we knew that this was our place. In all the details of the move to Manitoba, one song stayed with me continually: "Be still my soul...in every change, He faithful will remain."[17] I didn't realize the extent of the changes that we would experience.

Within a few months, we felt an undercurrent of questions regarding our style of leadership. What we were best known for was now questioned and criticized. The undercurrent grew to outright rejection, and the end result was that after one and a half years of ministry, we were asked to resign. Our call was aborted. It felt like a divorce. It was the most difficult time we had ever had in ministry. Dealing with rejection is deep and painful. We were in a life crisis!

## A NEW BEGINNING IS OFTEN DISGUISED AS A DIFFICULT END

Robert Clinton, in *The Making of a Leader*, defines a life crisis as an "intense pressure in which the meaning and purpose of life are searched out, with a result the leader has experienced God in a new way as the Source and Focus of Life."[18] My 50-year-old strong husband was now out of work, weak, vulnerable and afraid of the future. I was angry and worried about what would happen to us. My once happy home was now a place of sadness and depression. Tricia had great adjustments to make, including the loss of friends and enrolling in a new school. She fought depression and held

---

[17] Katharina A. von Schlegel, "Be Still My Soul," trans. Jane Borthwick, *The United Methodist Hymnal*, no. 534.

[18] Robert Clinton, *The Making of a Leader: Recognizing the Lessons and Stages of Leadership Development* (N.p.: NavPress, 1988), 164–165.

anger in her heart. To see her parents in this predicament after 12 years of wonderful ministry in Greenfield was too much for her heart.

Our son, Tim, and his college sweetheart, Kim, were married during this difficult time and soon relocated to Woodstock, Ontario, to take on a youth pastor position with an amazing pastor, Rev. Earl Young. Despite the joy of their wedding, we continued to grieve. I read everything I could on grief and loss. I understood that we had a choice of how to respond. Robert Clinton writes that processing a crisis can either drive leaders deeper into the presence of God or drive them away from God.[19] Whatever would happen to us in the future, I refused to become a living dead woman. I refused to carry anger and bitterness in my heart to embitter my family and future grandchildren. I refused to give my children a legacy of pain. We had to rise and live!

First and foremost was the work of releasing and dealing with negative toxic emotions. This, I learned, is very hard work. It takes mental and spiritual concentration to "take every thought captive to obey Christ" (2 Corinthians 10:5). Yet to fully live again, this was necessary. Like peeling an onion layer by layer, it took time.

One day on my prayer walk, I noted the clumps of dirty snow still left on the lawns. Crocuses had burst through the stubborn soil and were about to bloom. After a hard winter, the soil was yielding to spring and life—a resurrection. Immediately I became aware of a great spiritual lesson: whenever you go through a death-life experience, there has to be a resurrection. It was a God-moment, a direct revelation to my aching heart that we would rise. And we did!

After only a few months had passed, the largest United church in Brandon asked Bob to fill in for their minister, without any restrictions on sermon topics. He filled that pulpit many, many times. Other church denominations called and asked for his help. He was often double-booked, and so I helped.

Amazingly, God then opened up a small Free Methodist church for us in Killarney, Manitoba. This congregation of 18 to 20 people was God-given to bring us healing. I will never look down on a small church! Small churches have a large place in God's kingdom. This congregation loved us to health. The rich times of worship and the friendships we formed over many a meal bonded us to these rural people, who valued life, each other and us.

---

[19] Clinton, *The Making of a Leader*.

For an eight-year period we pastored the Killarney Free Methodist Church and accepted bookings at many other churches, keeping us both involved in Sunday ministry. Often we would pass each other on the highway, signalling a high-five. We felt blessed! This unexpected "pulpit-supply" ministry change taught us one big lesson: God's people are everywhere! Worship styles may differ, church forms and liturgy may differ, and church cultures may vary, but God has His people everywhere. It was very freeing to be part of God's bigger kingdom. It prepared me for my next season, which would come in a few years, with Women Alive!

Because of a loss of income, I again had to find work. God directed me to Seniors for Seniors, an organization that serviced some 4,000 seniors in Brandon and Western Manitoba. In my position as resource coordinator, I organized and planned all the programs and activities, including a weekly community TV program, a volunteer appreciation night at city hall and a health fair that drew over 1,500 people at its peak. Because of my profile in the city, I served on several community boards, including Westman Interfaith Counselling Centre, Brandon Seniors Housing Committee, Brandon Community Health Partners, YWCA Women of Distinction Awards, and the mayor's Volunteer Service Awards. These experiences helped me to learn about governance and financial accountability—another preparation for my future.

Most of my speaking invitations during this time came from secular organizations and community support groups. These leaders became my friends, and I learned about their caring hearts long before I learned about their faith or lack of faith. With my involvement in the community, I learned about the value placed on support groups as the caring component of the community. Churches, I saw, were on the perimeter and not at the centre of community life. They were largely unknown because they were perceived as separate entities not meeting the needs of the community.

A number of pastors in Brandon at that time had to leave their churches for one reason or another, and because I knew the pain, I went to the head of the local ministerial to ask if I could begin something for pastors' wives. He affirmed my request. I contacted several ministries for resources, one of which was Women Alive, led by Dr. Nell Maxwell. Dr. Maxwell had founded Women Alive in the early 1970s against a backdrop of social turmoil over issues such as the role of women. The purpose of the ministry was to equip and encourage Christian women to fulfill their

God-given calling. Under Nell's leadership, Women Alive impacted over half a million women. High-quality conferences were the primary means of ministry and were welcomed by women. This was an empowering ministry to women, many of whom went on to start their own ministries.

I had met Dr. Maxwell a number of years before through my friendship with Eileen Stewart Rhude, then the national women's ministry director for the Pentecostal Assemblies of Canada. Nell contacted me immediately and asked if I would develop Women Alive in Manitoba and Saskatchewan. I accepted. With Sunday pulpit supply and my work at Seniors for Seniors, this seemed a little out of control. But my heart was for women, and I longed to be back doing what I knew God had called me to do. From 1996 to 2000, I set up and developed planning teams and conferences in Brandon, Winnipeg, Regina, Kindersley and Saskatoon. In hindsight, if I had declined this invitation I would never have been asked to serve as the president of Women Alive. Our choices always lead us somewhere!

In July 2000, I was awarded the Paul Harris Award by Rotary International for community service in Brandon, Manitoba. The community honoured me. The song that God gave me when we were moving to Brandon came true! "In every change, He faithful will remain." Rejection does not mean failure, and neither does it mean an end. What seems as wrong, unfair and unjust is not the end of the story. It's just the end of a chapter. God allows even the very painful things to redirect us and move us on.

Bob and I learned more about the sovereignty of God during this 10-year period than in any other season of our 25 years in pastoral ministry. We learned to anchor into our calling because we were called not by men but by God. We learned that true and loyal friends always emerge in a life crisis and will give needed support. Those who really love and believe in you will be there. And we had them in various parts of Canada, including a very strong core in Brandon.

What we didn't realize at the time was that God was doing more then we saw or realized to prepare us and set up amazing connections for the next chapter of our lives. One such example involved our daughter, Tricia. She was invited to serve as the student youth pastor at First Baptist Church in Brandon. Little did we know that this was a foundation for her work today as student ministry pastor at Bethel Church in Sarnia, Ontario.

We also learned big lessons on forgiveness and trusting. The two are not the same. It's one thing to forgive and quite another to trust again. It has been said, "There comes a point in life when you realize who matters, who never did, who won't anymore, and who always will." Some people will never be a part of our future. I learned about the power of prayer and the working of God's Spirit to move us from venting and worry prayers to prayers of praise and worship and glorious heart freedom!

As we healed, adjusted and waited for our God's next plan to unfold, we noted God-moments and God-pointers that encouraged us to believe for more. My father's constant encouragement of "God will see you through" helped us to hope again. Hope, the immune system of the soul, was being restored in our lives!

Emotional upheaval is very difficult to deal with. Yet from a much higher perspective, no matter what unexpected changes and challenges we experience, God's love never diminishes, His grace never lessens, His anointing never lifts, His peace never fades and His faithfulness never falters. God will work to unfold His plan. It's only a matter of time.

God's promise to us remained: "I will lead the blind by ways they have not known, along unfamiliar paths I will guide them; I will turn the darkness into light before them and make the rough places smooth. These are the thing I will do; I will not forsake them" (Isaiah 42:16, NIV).

Our life-altering experience gave us much valuable knowledge. Today I reach out to people experiencing a tough end and transition. It's not the details that interest me; it's the recovery and moving on with life and calling. There's enough resurrection power in the heart of a believer to rise in the face of any tough circumstance! We may *believe* in resurrection, but as we rise we come to *understand* the power that is ours by what was accomplished by Christ in His death and resurrection.

## DEVELOPING LEADERS EMBRACE CHANGE

In mid-1998, I had a sense that change was coming. Bob and I often talked about this, but we didn't know what would open for us. My work with Women Alive in Manitoba and Saskatchewan was now much more fulfilling than my work in the community and with seniors. Would God open a door to work only with women to fulfill His call back in 1978? I didn't know, but I knew where my heart was. In late 1999, I received three good job offers, one of which was for the seniors' directorate in Winnipeg.

I was expected to make a decision for each offer within a 10-day period. Bob and I prayed and felt that we should decline each offer and wait.

Unexpectedly, the board of directors at Women Alive approached me in February 2000 about my interest to follow Dr. Nell Maxwell as president. The board was embarking on a Canada-wide search for the "right leader." I felt safe to submit my name only because I felt underqualified compared to the many outstanding women who could fill the role of president. I didn't think my application would go very far in the process. The step up to being president of a national women's organization seemed premature for me. Yet the adventure to try called me!

To my surprise, I made the short list. That's when I knew that this was serious and required much prayer. For six months, we went back and forth to work out many details, and, finally, in October 2000, I accepted the invitation to be president of Women Alive.

When I arrived in the office in Barrie, Ontario, for my first day, January 3, 2001, a bouquet of roses greeted me with a note from Bob: "If anyone can do it, you're the one!" I still carry that card in my wallet!

When I accepted the role of president, apart from the call of God, I had more against me than for me! To follow a founder is always challenging. I had big shoes to fill, and I was an unknown. "Margaret who?" was often said. I came from Manitoba, not the ministry hub of Toronto. I didn't know any Christian ministry leaders, and I didn't know the staff or donors at Women Alive. With limited fundraising experience I had to cast a fresh vision and bring vitality back to this needed ministry. I often quoted Robert Browning from "Andrea del Sarto" during this time: "A man's reach should exceed his grasp,/ Or what's a heaven for?"

My first year was probably the hardest. Our house in Brandon needed to be sold, so I commuted by air from Brandon to Barrie every few weeks, living with three different families for a period of 14 months. The board decided to move the office to Brantford, and new staff had to be hired. Teams needed encouragement, funds needed to be raised, and I needed to "win" the constituency. It was a stressful year, yet many miracles happened along the way, including the donation of a new Impala, which encouraged the board and me that we were moving in the right direction.

My ten years with Women Alive were rich with team building, program development and collaboration with an incredible core that believed in the ministry and its impact on women. The regional chairs were amazing women doing a great work across Canada. Vinetta Sanderson, Ellen Wells, Ruth Coghill, Caroline Laing, Eileen Stewart Rhude, Marilyn Bussey and the late Ruth Bauman Code were a powerhouse team. Together we dreamed, prayed, solved challenges, travelled throughout Canada and made incredible memories. Pages of stories could be written on the miracles we witnessed and the impact that Women Alive had on women.

In 2005, a banner year, Women Alive hosted 38 conferences. Our finances grew. We had momentum. Besides annual conferences, we began the i.e. girl program for teen girls and *Women Alive*, a magazine for Canadian Christian women, with Karen Stiller as editor. We hosted *Leading Edge*, a leadership development training program for women, we partnered with Precept Ministries in a special conference called Just the Word, and we worked with FaithLife Financial to develop the Debt-Free Woman program.

Amidst all of this activity, I continued to write. I wrote many articles for *Maranatha News, Christian Herald*, and, later, *Christian Week*. In total, over 60 articles were published in this period, reaching a national audience. The prophetic word given over me as a young girl in Edmonton, Alberta, was being fulfilled.

Three things happened during my ten years in Women Alive that indicated the coming new season. The first indicator was my surrender to Africa. I had told God at age 16 that I would never set foot on that continent, but in 2003 I accepted—with much trepidation—an invitation from World Vision to join a delegation of clergy and leaders to visit Uganda and Tanzania to see first-hand the effect of HIV and AIDS on women and children. Seeing that suffering changed me forever. We visited child-headed households, spoke with grandmothers raising more than 13 grandchildren, and sat with single moms suffering with HIV or AIDS. I knew that this was only the beginning of my involvement with Africa.

The second indicator was a growing desire to empower women internationally. As I travelled the nation representing Women Alive, I met experienced nurses, teachers, doctors, nutritionists, dental hygienists and speakers who wanted to do more with their skills and resources to help women in developing countries. I saw an opportunity to channel the resources of these professionals to women in need in other countries. A large vision-seed was planted in my heart, and it continued to grow. While my vision grew, I was in inner conflict, because the firm stand of Women Alive was that it would be a Canada-only ministry. Overseas missions were not something the ministry had as its mandate. I didn't know how the future would unfold. I just knew that a new vision was developing in me.

The third indicator was a heartbreak that shifted my whole world. In March 2007, I joined my son, Tim, and my daughter, Tricia, at a pastors' conference in Fort Portal, Uganda. Bob had not been well for several years leading up to this trip. He was in the hospital at the time, but we didn't suspect that his illness was anything serious. We went to Uganda with his full blessing and the doctor's approval. Africa was a place Bob always wanted to visit but never did. That the three were in Uganda together brought him much joy. As a family, we were doing ministry as a team!

We talked to Bob every day while we were away and communicated with the nursing staff daily. On March 5, in a smelly, crammed Internet café in downtown Nairobi, we heard of his passing. We were shocked and heartbroken.

Isaiah 66:13–14 became our comfort: "'As a mother comforts her child, so will I comfort you; and you will be comforted...' When you see this, your heart will rejoice and you will flourish like grass; the hand of the LORD will be made known to his servants" (NIV).

I wrestled with great guilt and sadness, but Chris Tomlin's song "How Great Is Our God" sprung up within me and did not go away for months.

After Bob's passing, something shifted in my love and passion for Women Alive. The desire to plan more conferences was gone. Often I would think, *How many more times do Canadian Christian women need to be told that they have a God-given purpose? Why is there a need to bolster self-worth and reiterate purpose when we live in one of the richest countries in the world? Yes, we do matter and we have a purpose, but shouldn't that message stir us to step out and engage with women living in other cultures, who also matter and have a purpose?*

I remember asking one day at a meeting with our graphic designer and staff, "What's the popular font right now? What are the in-colours for this season?" As I was asking these kinds of questions, I knew that the needs of women in developing countries were of much greater concern for me. I had to move on.

The name "Women Together" came to me two years before I resigned from Women Alive. I envisioned Canadian Christian women, seasoned

and experienced, coming alongside women in developing countries to provide education, leadership training, tools, skills development and biblical instruction. I pictured teams of nurses, teachers and speakers offering their help with teaching aid materials, medical clinics and leadership training to equip women. I envisioned a global community of Christian women living fully in Jesus Christ, serving others and mutually learning from each other. By investing in women in developing countries we Canadian women, I believed, would be making the greatest investment possible. And why not? We had the resources. As days went on, my dream grew stronger and stronger. I became pregnant with a new call.

In the fall of 2008, just over a year after my husband's passing and six months after my dear father's entry to heaven, there was a downturn in the economy that greatly affected Women Alive, a ministry dependent on income from conference registrations. Staff layoffs became necessary, and I was devastated to have to face this reality. I wept hard at this needed change. It was another huge loss. Having to release excellent staff is one of the hardest experiences in leadership.

At this very difficult time we had specific days of prayer and fasting with staff and focused on the book *The Red Sea Rules: 10 God-Given Strategies for Difficult Times* by Robert J. Morgan.[20] The tag line reads, "The same God who led you in will lead you out." We worked through the layoffs and knew that even in this time of hardship God had a plan. Together we were led in; together we were being led out. This proved to be true, as our wonderful friendships continue to this day!

Emotionally, I was very drained. I was in burnout and knew it! Someone recommended a timely book that helped me immensely, Wayne Cordeiro's *Leading on Empty*. I starred and underlined these words: "Each of us has an internal and emotional reservoir. On the topside there's an input, and on the bottom, a drain. Certain activities will drain you more than fill you, and others will fill you more than drain you. Some tasks will contribute to you and others will take from you."[21] Wayne Cordeiro posed two questions that I needed to answer: "What fills you?" and "What drains you?" I knew that for too long my emotional reservoir had

---

[20] Robert J. Morgan, *The Red Sea Rules: 10 God-Given Strategies for Difficult Times* (Nashville: Thomas Nelson Publishers, 2001).

[21] Wayne Cordeiro, *Leading on Empty: Refilling Your Tank and Renewing Your Passion* (Minneapolis: Bethany House, 2009), 89.

been depleted because I was not working in my giftings. I needed to fuel my new dream!

I resigned from Women Alive in September 2009 and officially ended my time in December 2010. God gave me 10 wonderful years of connection, growth and development. I continue to be incredibly thankful for the privilege I had to lead this ministry and serve the women of Canada.

With faith and passion, I now could pursue my new dream—Women Together, an international ministry that would create a global community of Christian women who live to glorify God and serve others. Vision has only one focus—forward. I would not be chained to my past. I would take the steps to move forward and with God's help create something new and fresh internationally and call it Women Together. Every season is a preparation for the next one. Women Alive prepared me for Women Together.

I applied for charity status in May 2011, and approval came in October 2011. I was off and running! A short sabbatical of rest, reflection, planning and dreaming gave me time to focus on my next adventure.

My first mission trip with Women Together was to Ukraine, a place that was never on my radar even as a possibility. When I stepped on the soil of Ukraine in November 2010, I felt humbled and nervous at the same time. I was in my ancestral home—the country where my grandparents and parents were born. Would I belong? Would I feel a connection with the women? Would my Ukrainian background be received even though I didn't speak the language or understand the culture?

I made my way up a flight of stairs to the auditorium where my first women's conference was to be held. Worship music filled the air. Four beautiful Ukrainian women were singing "Shout to the Lord" in the language of my ancestors! Even though I didn't understand the words, I understood their hearts. Tears filled my eyes. I knew I belonged.

When I got up to speak, I began by telling the women about my grandfather, who was orphaned at 10 years of age, and about his difficult life. I shared about his remarkable conversion to Christ and his three-year prison term because of his faith. I told them how miraculously my grandfather received his theological training in prison, which prepared him for ministry in Canada.

"Now, three generations later, I am with you," I said to the women. "I serve the same God as my grandfather. I love Jesus and believe in His power to transform a life. I am here because of a generational calling. I am here to work with the women of Ukraine."

Women Together is a growing global ministry for women, involved in Kenya, Uganda, Ukraine, Brazil and India and the Philippines. Under the direction of Patricia Klein, Women Together organizes two or three teams each year to provide overseas ministry and medical assistance through health care training, wellness clinics, leadership training, women's conferences, retreats for pastors' wives and schools of leadership. We are now established in Ukraine and Kenya with national coordinators Veronika Nuzhna and Eunice Monda in place. Women Together in Ukraine publishes an e-magazine for Ukrainian and Russian women that now reaches into 26 countries of the world.

Judy Rushfeldt coordinates our global leadership webinars, providing online leadership training, mentoring for women leaders and more recently online women's conferences in places like Pakistan.

Our scholarship program, We Were Made for More, focuses on women in developing countries who are enrolled in a BA, BTh or MDiv program from an accredited college. We financially support young women in Brazil, Kenya and India.

In our nation of Canada, we are hosting and organizing peer care retreats, personal times of refreshing and empowerment for women in leadership. Ruth Coghill gives oversight to this needed and growing program and other initiatives.

Can God call and use a shy, introverted girl, locked in a self-inflicted prison, and develop her to direct a global ministry? Absolutely yes!

"Before I formed you in the womb I knew you, before you were born I set you apart; I appointed you" (Jeremiah 1:4–5, NIV).

There are no shortcuts or 10 easy steps in leadership development. All seasons, stages and tests work together to ultimately achieve God's plan and purposes. When I first committed myself to ministry and marriage, I thought life would move in a straight line. It didn't. Experience can be a brutal teacher. Every experience in life adds to the development story. It is only when we look back that we can connect the dots and see God at work. It was Søren Kierkegaard who said, "Life can only be understood backwards; but it must be lived forwards."[22]

---

[22] Paraphrase of Søren Kierkegaard, *Journalen* JJ:167, *Søren Kierkegaards Skrifter*, Søren Kierkegaard Research Center, Copenhagen, 1997, volume 18 (1843), 306.

In 1980 when I started journaling, I chose Psalm 32:8 as my life verse: "I will instruct you and teach you in the way you should go; I will counsel you with my loving eye on you" (NIV). This verse has been my anchor and one I pray almost daily!

In mentoring women in leadership, I often offer some basic principles I have learned:

1. The greatest achievement you ever attain in life is in hearing the call of God and fulfilling your God-given purpose. Nothing is more important.

2. Anchor into your calling. It is for your lifetime and will keep you. It is the bedrock of your leadership and character development.

3. Accept your uniqueness and personal design as God's gift to you. Be yourself. Don't compare yourself to others. It will profit you nothing.

4. Leadership and character development is a long journey. Give it the time it takes. Don't rush the seasons. Each season has its own rhythm, tests and learning curves. Flow with what God is teaching you.

5. Seldom does God promote a leader quickly. Responsibility has to match character. Potential is one thing. Potential, character and experience are quite another.

6. Vision never unveils; it unfolds. Be totally dependent on the Holy Spirit. Listen for His voice and promptings. He will teach you lessons that you cannot otherwise learn. He will show you your next steps.

7. Surround yourself with mentors and faith-filled people. No leader is self-made. Draw from others' years of experience and wisdom.

8. Be a reader. Leaders are readers. Effective leaders have a drive to learn and maintain a learning posture throughout their lifetime.

9. Ensure that spiritual disciplines are the "first of the first" in importance. Being in the Word, growing in prayer and worship and journaling are all part of developing a deeper dependent relationship on God. There is no way to learn to pray but by praying. Spiritual disciplines feed the soul, form character and deepen spiritual maturity.

10. You will make mistakes and even fail. In development there has to be room for failure. Where there is no failure, there will be no growth. Learn and move on.

11. Let God promote you, in His way, in His time. Wait. Don't strive. When you get there, the door will open.

12. Be faithful! The yardstick of faithfulness measures leadership and character maturity.

13. Don't miss the miracles along the way! Mark down the God-moments and God-markers. They will be your source of encouragement, the basis of many stories and a legacy of your journey with God.

Henry Blackaby in *Experiencing God* wrote, "Anything significant that happens in our life will be a result of God's activity in life."[23] To be chosen, called and commissioned by God is only the first step in fulfilling what God has called us to do. The daily dependence on God in the journey will ultimately take us into places of leadership we never dreamed of. "The one who calls you is faithful, and he will do it" (1 Thessalonians 5:24, NIV).

---

 Margaret Gibb is the founder and executive director of Women Together, an international women's ministry. Margaret has worked with women since 1978 when the call and passion to see women rise to their full potential and fulfill their God-given calling were deeply embedded in her heart. A mentor, motivator and encourager, Margaret is a champion of women wherever they live and regardless of their circumstances. She believes that "God's women empowered by His Spirit can change the world."

In 2014, Margaret was selected as one of Canada's 100 Christian women leaders by Bridgeway Foundation. She is a sought-after speaker across Canada. Margaret has two adult children: Tim, lead pastor of Bethel Church, Sarnia, Ontario, and Tricia, student ministry pastor at the same church. Margaret is ordained with the Pentecostal Assemblies of Canada.

---

[23] Henry Blackaby, *Experiencing God* (Nashville: Broadman & Holman Publishers, 1994), 6.